Relief
Woodcarving

E.J. Tangerman

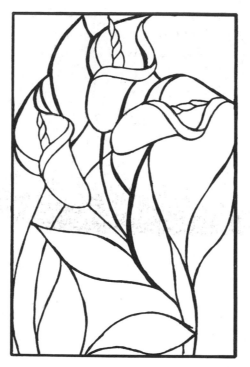

Sterling Publishing Co., Inc. New York

Other books by E. J. Tangerman

Capturing Personality in Woodcarving
Carving Faces and Figures in Wood
Carving Flora and Fables in Wood
Carving Religious Motifs in Wood
Carving Wooden Animals

Library of Congress Cataloging in Publication Data
Tangerman, E. J. (Elmer John), 1907–
  Relief woodcarving.

  (Home craftsman series)
  Includes index.
  1. Wood-carving.   I. Title.   II. Series.
TT199.7.T374   736′.4   81-85039
ISBN 0-8069-7596-2 (pbk.)   AACR2

Copyright © 1981 by Sterling Publishing Co., Inc.
Two Park Avenue, New York, N.Y. 10016
Distributed in Australia by Oak Tree Press Co., Ltd.
P.O. Box J34, Brickfield Hill, Sydney 2000, N.S.W.
Distributed in the United Kingdom by Blandford Press
Link House, West Street, Poole, Dorset BH15 1LL, England
Distributed in Canada by Oak Tree Press Ltd.
c/o Canadian Manda Group, 215 Lakeshore Boulevard East
Toronto, Ontario M5A 3W9
Manufactured in the United States of America
All rights reserved
Library of Congress Catalog Card No.: 81-85039
Sterling ISBN 0-8069-7596-2

Contents

Fig. 1. Wide low-relief panels of local scenes face the balconies of a hotel in Puerto Moutt, Chile.

The "Why" of Relief Woodcarving

FOR OVER FIFTY YEARS, I HAVE BEEN FASCINATED by the infinite possibilities of relief carving, ranging from geometric patterns on to portraits and full-fledged scenes. A relief carving need not be a flat, rectangular panel; it can be a silhouette with or without pierced elements that allow light or the background to show through in parts. It can be wrapped around a non-planar shape such as a cylinder, a ball, a log or even a shape as irregular as a wooden shoe. It can incorporate inlays, utilize the grain or "figure" of the wood, suggest a texture, be a simple study of a small subject or a complex treatment of an involved one. It is almost as flexible as in-the-round carving, since the third dimension can suit the wood and the subject, with the added advantage of letting you hold elements together, provide a scene or background and protect the piece against undue wear or damage. It can be traditional or modern, realistic or abstract, even "inside-out" as an intaglio or a mould. And it can be painted or stained, but usually does not need to be, thus retaining the natural warmth of the wood. In short, relief carving can tell almost any story you want it to, from a mere feeling to the setting of an entire scene, or even several scenes one within the other.

All of my books have contained numerous relief carvings, but none have yet been devoted expressly to relief itself. Here, then, is a wide variety of relief-carved projects, graded for difficulty and not repeated elsewhere. They include my own work and that of selected carvers around the world, to show the tremendous range and possibilities in this form. Also included are the basics of wood, tools, lettering, sharpening and finishing, as well as patterns and hints piece by piece. This book should meet the needs of both the beginner and the skilled craftsman. I wish you well!

E. J. Tangerman

CHAPTER I

What Wood Is Best?

GENERALLY SPEAKING, THE GAMUT OF WOODS has been used in relief carving, sometimes because a wood was readily available or easily carved, sometimes because it was the right color, texture, pattern, had some significance or even rarity. Panels in churches have usually been carved in local woods such as walnut, pine, basswood, maple, butternut, cherry and apple in the United States; oak, lime, linden, apple and deal (fir or pine) in Europe; and in Egypt, sycamore and cedar. Panels carved for furniture have varied with fashion. Cherry wasn't used until 1675, mahogany didn't appear in Europe in any quantity until 1720 and teak came into use much more recently.

In the United States, the familiar woods for relief carving are black walnut, mahogany, cherry and other fruit woods; for signs or painted outdoor units, basswood and white pine are the usual choices. I have carved all of these, as well as teak, butternut, maple, pear, pecan, ash, vermilion, purpleheart, ebony and others. But for practical purposes, including available sizes and ease of working, I prefer pine, basswood, cherry, walnut and teak. Use walnut, mahogany, cherry and teak for relief work not to be painted. For exterior work, teak is superior because it does not rot or warp, and is not prone to insect attack.

Many of the exotic woods so familiar for veneering, such as avodire, satin, beef, purpleheart, greenheart, zebra and the African woods in general, are hard to carve because they split, have irregular grain or create other problems. The typical relief carving is a panel. Thus, wood should be straight-grained, so backgrounding and modelling can both be done well, without too much "figure," grain or knots, which compete with the carving, and without too much tendency to warp, splinter and split. It should also be dense enough to support detail, and preferably hard enough not to be worn away by cleaning and polishing through the years.

The color of a particular wood will sometimes suggest its use, such as myrtle for a mask, vermilion for a small award panel and purpleheart for an unusual subject such as a Celtic bird. But if you plan to carve in a wood with which you have no experience, try a sample before getting started on the general project. In most instances, I have indicated the woods used for the carvings pictured and described herein. Depending upon your experience with a wood, you may want to simplify the proposed design, or alter the arrangement to put a knot or flaw in an unimportant spot.

For any larger panels these days, it is usually necessary to assemble the panel from milled boards. On darker woods without conspicuous grain— walnut, mahogany, teak—the joining lines can be made to disappear almost entirely. They must, however, have smooth-planed edges for good joints, and should preferably be dowelled, glued and clamped to assure tightness. The wood should also be relatively thick; ½- and 1-in (13- and 25.4-mm) panels of pine, walnut and mahogany tend to warp and move with the weather regardless of finish. If you anticipate or encounter appreciable warpage, brace the back of the panel with screwed-on battens across-grain, or with angle irons or aluminum angles. I have used the latter in a number of instances, even to assemble a walnut mailbox of ½-in (13-mm) wood, carved on surfaces and edges. It has held for ten years, completely exposed (with marine-varnish finish). I have also seen thick relief carvings a hundred or more years old in which the center of the back was hollowed appreciably to counteract warpage, just as old-time in-the-round figures were split and hollowed out to avoid checking.

CHAPTER II

Some Suggestions on Tools

Buy them as you need them, not for stock

THE KNIFE IS THE MOST VERSATILE of woodcarving tools and works fine for carving relatively small or hand-sized pieces in-the-round; but it does have limitations in making larger pieces and cutting concave or intaglio surfaces. Some adaptations of blade shapes have been made, such as hooks and spoons, but they have only limited capacity. Though I am a life-long knife user, I must admit that there are projects for which only chisels make sense. These include almost all relief carving, unless it is silhouettes or pierced work—which is essentially flattened in-the-round carving.

This does not mean that the knife is abandoned in relief. Far from it. I find it most reliable for details and hard-to-reach places. It does mean, however, that you should have available half a dozen or so chisels and some way of holding the work securely. This is because the chisel is driven by arm rather than hand muscles, making force and length of stroke less controllable on many cuts. Also, tool selection and maintenance become more important.

Because relief carving is less portable in most instances than whittling, you don't really need a pocketknife at all; you can work quite well with a fixed-blade carver's knife in any of several shapes, as seen in figure 2. I use a fairly standard one. In either case, however, you need a good point. As to chisels, this will depend a good deal upon what you are planning to carve, whether it is small or large, simple or involved, with large surfaces or small ones. Generally speaking, small tools can be used on large carvings but large tools may not be useful on small ones. In fact, professional carvers in under-developed countries, who have only a few tools, tend to have small-bladed ones—often without handles—and only a club for a mallet. They take more cuts but reduce the risk of breakage.

Carver's chisels have been made and used for so long that they have their own special terminology. The flat chisel, like a carpenter's but thinner and sharpened from both sides so it doesn't dig, is called a *firmer* (see sketches). If the edge is sharpened at an angle, it is a *skew firmer*; if the corners of the edge are rounded, it is called a *bullnose* and can actually be used for many of the same operations as a flat gouge. Then there is the *V-tool* or *parting tool*, which is really two firmers joined at an angle (usually acute) along one side, for cutting a V-groove in a single pass. Variations of this tool rarely seen nowadays are the *macaroni*, which cuts a flat-bottomed trench, and the *fluteroni*, which makes a similar groove with rounded corners.

The workhorse tools of the woodcarver are the gouges—curved-edge tools that come in a bewildering array of shapes and sizes. These range from the *veiner*, with a half-circle cross section that can be as small as $\frac{1}{32}$ or $\frac{1}{16}$ in (.8 or 1.6 mm) across inside, through the *fluter*, similar but U-shaped in cross section, to large and very flat gouges up to 2½ in (6.4 cm) wide. In Europe, tools are sized by millimeters: 1, 2, 3, 4, 5, 6, 7, 8, 10, 12, 16, 20, 25, 30, etc. The arc of a gouge is called the *sweep*, commonly referred to by number according to the "London (or English) system." Thus a firmer is No. 1, a skew firmer 2, a flat gouge 3 and a semicircular one 11 or 12. (Some suppliers also assign numbers to special tools.)

Wide tools, and some narrower ones, are tapered down to the tang (which enters the handle) to reduce weight and increase versatility by giving greater clearance. These are called *spade* or *fishtail* tools. The shank may also be bent into a long arc (*long-bent*) or a short one (*short-bent*) to get the cutting edge into tight places. Some gouges are even bent backwards, known as *back-bent* tools. Small tools, such as an engraver's burin, are also made with short shanks and palm handles. They are fine for close work but cannot be used with the mallet, thus limiting their usefulness. Bent tools and palm tools are usually not required for simple relief carving; I rarely use them. The bent tools are harder to sharpen and tend to spring in use.

Carving tools may be pushed by hand in softer woods, in which case they are pushed with one hand, guided and restrained with the other. Thus the work should be held in some way, either in a vise, by a carver's screw (which goes through the workbench into the bottom of the workpiece) or, if it is a panel, by a clamp or on a benchplate (Fig. 6). I have nailed a panel to the bench through the waste wood or put it on a rubber doormat.

The regular mallet is shaped like an old-fashioned potato masher, usually in a hard and heavy wood like cocobola, and is available in various weights;

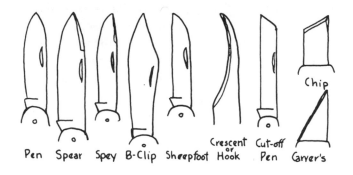

Pen Spear Spey B-Clip Sheepfoot Crescent or Hook Cut-off Pen Carver's Chip

Fig. 2. Knife blades.

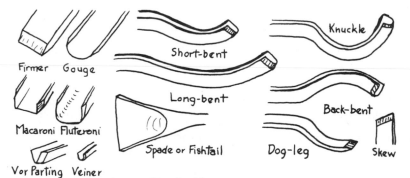

Firmer Gouge Short-bent Knuckle

Macaroni Fluteroni Long-bent Back-bent

Spade or Fishtail Dog-leg Skew

Vor Parting Veiner

Fig. 3. Chisel shapes.

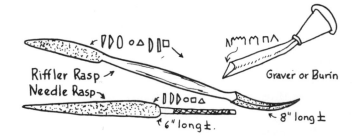

Riffler Rasp
Needle Rasp

Graver or Burin

6" long ±.

8" long ±

Fig. 4. Rasps and burin.

I've seen them up to 5 or 6 lb (2.3 or 2.7 kg). In these inventive days there are mallets cast of babbitt metal, turned from aluminum and made from old washing-machine wringer rolls and soft-faced hammers. In recent years, I have been using vinyl-faced ones—they're easier on my arthritis. I find that I can control the cut much better with a mallet than without.

There are also endless variations in tools, suiting the preferences of individuals or groups. H. M. Sutter, who has taught carving for over 40 years, has recently developed thin tools less likely to wedge and splinter the wood when setting-in is done (see the next chapter for Mr. Sutter's designs). Totem-pole and wooden-Indian carvers use chain saws, sometimes exclusively, while others prefer rotary grinders and flexible-shaft units equipped with cutters. I met one carver who uses a pneumatic or electric hammer, others who use belt sanders, circular saws, bandsaws or what have you. The principal intention in most of these cases is to get rid of the waste wood quickly, which is usually not a great problem in relief carving. Rotary tools can be used, but in my experience they tend to run, tear and burn the wood, and require such safety equipment as goggles and respirators. I do, however, use a router when I have large areas of background to cut down.

What tools to buy initially depends largely on what you plan to make and your personal preference. I seldom use more than ten tools, even on my most complicated carvings, but this may vary with the size of the work. I started with a kit of nine tools, about three of which I have hardly ever used. Charles M. Sayers, who taught panel carving, suggested five initial tools: ⅜- to ½-in (9.5- to 13-mm) or ⅝-in (16-mm) No. 39 parting or V-tool; ⅝-in (16-mm) No. 5 straight gouge; ⅞- or 1-in (22.4- or 25.4-mm) No. 3 straight gouge; ⅜-in (9.5-mm) No. 7 straight gouge; and a ⅜-in (9.5-mm) No. 3 straight gouge. H. M. Sutter also starts his students with five, plus an all-purpose knife: ⅜-in (9.5-mm) No. 3 straight gouge and a ⅝-in (16-mm) No. 5 straight gouge (these two preferably fishtail); ⅜-in (9.5-mm) No. 9 straight gouge; ⅟₁₆- or ⅟₃₂-in (1.6- or .8-mm) No. 11 veiner; and a ⁵⁄₁₆- or ⅜-in (8- or 9.5-mm) parting or V-tool. My advice is to start with a similarly limited set and add tools as you need them, regardless of salesmen's suggestions. As you add tools, vary size and sweep considerably, and buy carpenter's chisels and gouges for big and rough work—they're cheaper and can take a beating. Beware, however, of patternmaker's gouges, which are sharpened inside on the concave surface.

It is easier to use chisels than knives, in my opinion, and faster on much work. When pounding, you must learn not to watch the handle but the cutting edge and to hold the mallet or chisel in either hand. Take it easy; don't try to remove all the waste wood in the first pass. In cross-grain cutting, start at an edge and work in. Don't work to the edge—you'll split out wood if you do. Keep the tools very sharp, or they'll tear wood on diagonal cuts. Soft woods require sharper tools than hard woods. Don't wedge out chips; cut them out. Don't use chisels to open paint cans or strip insulation off wires. Store them so the edges are protected—you can buy or make carrying rolls for this purpose.

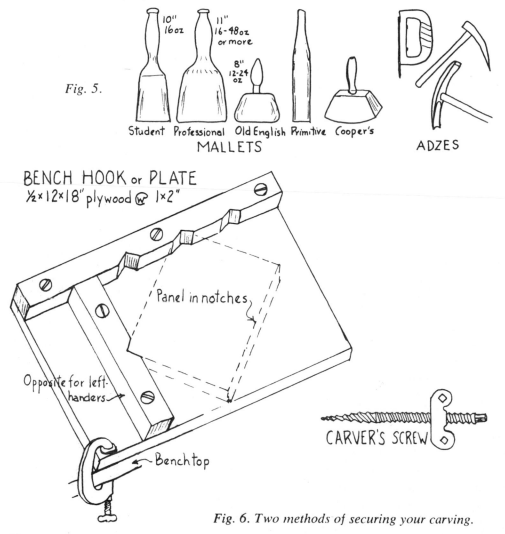

Fig. 5.

Student Professional Old English Primitive Cooper's
MALLETS

ADZES

BENCH HOOK or PLATE
½×12×18" plywood ⓦ 1×2"

Panel in notches

Opposite for left-handers

Benchtop

CARVER'S SCREW

Fig. 6. Two methods of securing your carving.

CHAPTER III

Thin Tools Speed Setting-In

Some typical Sutter designs and ideas

H. M. SUTTER HAS MADE HIS OWN thin-bladed tools for some years because he found them better and more convenient to use on small panels. They make setting-in, particularly around curves, quicker and easier by reducing the wedging action—hence the crushing and splitting of fibres—and the number of steps. And, small tools are less clumsy for intricate work. Such tools work just as well as heavier chisels for grounding out, but are not as safe for digging or prying—which we shouldn't do anyway. Nor will they stand mallet pounding as well as the heavier chisels, though they can be used with a soft- or plastic-faced mallet. They are lighter, cheaper and less fatiguing to hold, particularly when compared to some American tools, which are much too thick in smaller sizes.

Mr. Sutter has recently found a commercial company willing to make his style of tool, so beginner sets are now available. Each consists of six tools: a firmer ¼ in (6.4 mm) wide, and gouges of ¹⁄₁₆-, ⅛-, ³⁄₁₆-, ¼- and ⁵⁄₁₆-in (1.6-, 3.2-, 5-, 6.4- and 8-mm) width, all No. 7 sweep. The second set has No. 7 ⅜- to ⅝-in (9.5- 16-mm) gouges and a ⅝-in (16-mm) firmer.

He rounds off the heel on each gouge and increases the length of the bevel on the firmer to make true thin blades, which allow for deeper cuts without crushing. He also reports that such tools have made a considerable difference in the quality of the work done by his students, as well as the complexity they can handle. The pine-cone design was a real challenge, even for an advanced student, but can now be done with relative ease. The same is true for the more difficult orchid design. Large curves are cut with an all-purpose knife or with larger chisels if they are available. Students have also found that this kind of tool is quite satisfactory for carving in-the-round pieces.

Several of Mr. Sutter's patterns and finished pieces are pictured here. More basic designs are shown and described in my earlier book, *Carving Flora and Fables in Wood.* My students at Brasstown, North Carolina, usually skilled as whittlers but newly introduced to chisels, have done the designs shown there and here quite successfully.

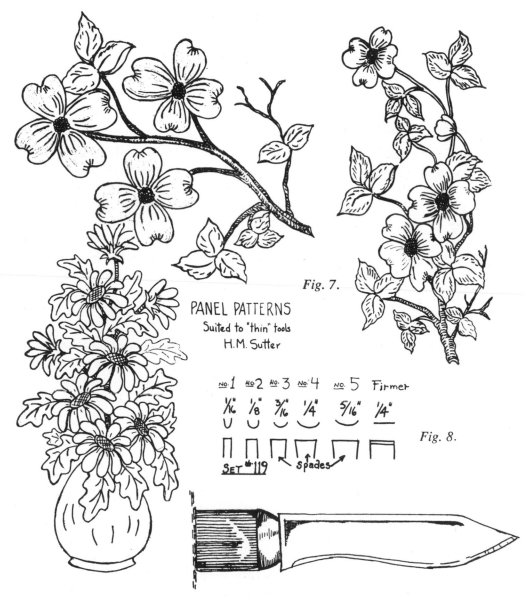

Fig. 7.

PANEL PATTERNS
Suited to "thin" tools
H.M. Sutter

NO. 1   NO. 2   NO. 3   NO. 4   NO. 5   Firmer
1/16"   1/8"   3/16"   1/4"   5/16"   1/4"

SET #119   ← Spades →

Fig. 8.

Fig. 9. All-purpose knife.

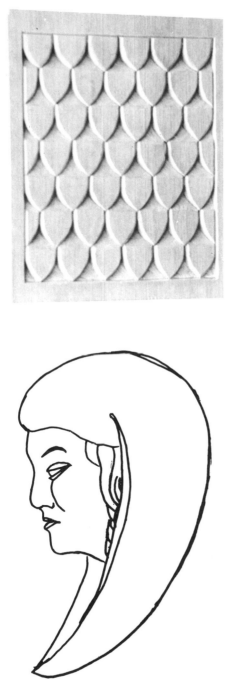

Fig. 10. Panel of overlapping simple shapes is a good exercise in setting-in and grounding. Lower portion of each leaf is sloped in to outline the next leaf shape. Conventional thick chisels would split the leaves apart in such a design.

Figs. 11–12 (above and left). This simple head can be raised above a background, trenched or silhouetted. Modelling is shallow but precise; thus, the project is more difficult than it appears to be. This is a good exercise in using the V-tool.

Figs. 13–14 (left and below). Three pine cones are another good subject for thin-bladed tools because of the overlapping seeds. Such designs should be trenched, with trenching sloping up to the surface all around, so needles can be cut into the surface with a V-tool. A groove can replace a raised rib here with no loss of realism.

Figs. 15–16. Simple group of stylized jack-in-the-pulpits, an Art Nouveau design. Stems are V-grooves.

Fig. 17. Head of a carousel horse is difficult to carve accurately in relief because of its twist. Although the eye is correctly positioned for in-the-round carving, it appears high and too far forward here.

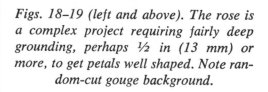

Figs. 18–19 (left and above). The rose is a complex project requiring fairly deep grounding, perhaps ½ in (13 mm) or more, to get petals well shaped. Note random-cut gouge background.

Figs. 20–21 (above and right). Most diffi-cult of the group is this double orchid, which requires as much as ¾ in (19 mm) of grounding to achieve the various levels and get the crenellations in the petals.

CHAPTER IV

An Introduction to Relief Carving

Definitions, techniques, shapes, finishes and backgrounds

CARVING IN RELIEF IS A VERSATILE approach and can offer many more possibilities than carving in-the-round, particularly when producing a legend or lettering a panel—the basics of which are covered in Chapters 16 and 17. Thus it is essential for signs, furniture, mouldings, framing and diaper patterns. It has traditionally been at least as familiar as in-the-round carving, but is less common in America where so many carvers are primarily knife whittlers. (And the knife is not the best tool for concave surfaces, part of many elements of panels.) There are also those who find relief carving to be more difficult than three-dimensional full figures, because the third dimension must be foreshortened and perspective may be involved. Further, if a regular geometric or other pattern is carved, it is easier to avoid making mistakes than it is trying to correct them. An error in an in-the-round figure, especially a caricature, is likely to go unnoticed, but an error in formal-pattern relief carving is likely to be quite visible.

Relief carving was originally just the scraping or incising of lines depicting something, probably at first on cave walls and then on wooden tools and the like. The Egyptians developed this into trench carving, which is simply digging a trench in the surface around a subject and modelling the subject itself in low relief so that no part of the design stands above the background panel level. In medieval Europe, however, and in some other areas of the world, relief carving progressed until it was sometimes extremely elaborate and might incorporate in-the-round elements or a close approximation of them.

Relief carving was thus classified by the Italians: High relief or *alto-relievo* carries projection from the background to half or more of the natural thickness of the subject. Some parts may be undercut or completely free of the background. In low relief, *basso-relievo* or *bas-relief*, the projection is slight and no parts are undercut or detached. Less commonly defined are half relief (*mezzo-relievo*) and the very flat relief of medals and coins called *stiacciato*. Hollow relief, also called *cavo-relievo, intaglio-relevato*, coelanaglyphic sculpture or simply trench carving, is that in which the background is not cut away; the figure or object being carved is outlined by a deep groove but has no elements higher than the background. This technique is effective for coats of arms, monograms, initials, lettering and other carving on a flat surface, particularly if it may be damaged by bumping or abrasion. This is not to be confused with intaglio, which is most easily described as reversed relief.

Fig. 22. Detail from a massive door in the Cathedral of Seville exemplifies high-relief style of former centuries. Note that female figures and floral swags between them are practically in-the-round.

In intaglio carving, the design is hollowed out so that material pressed or poured into it comes out as an image in relief. The most familiar objects in intaglio are cookie and butter moulds. When a pattern is pressed into sand to create a mould for metal, the mould itself is an intaglio. This is not a cameo, which is normally limited to a head or bust carved in multilayered stone or shell so that the carving is in one color, the background in another. However, a head or bust carved through a surface layer of one color into a differing color beneath, so that not only color change but reversal of the depths is attained, is an intaglio and a cameo.

A figure becomes in the round only when the third dimension is correct.

21

Fig. 23. Alonso Berruguete's life-size head of John the Baptist projects from this walnut panel in the Cathedral of Toledo.

Thus, a dog or horse carved in silhouette but flattened in body thickness is still relief carving, as is pierced carving, regardless of whether it contains in-the-round elements. The same is true of high relief, which often contains foreground figures cut free of the background; they may be in the round themselves but are still part of a relief carving. I have done relief carving on trees, bowls, napkin rings and even on wooden shoes. These are, in a sense, three-dimensional, as is a mobile made up of relief silhouettes. It is possible to have two relief carvings on opposite sides of the same silhouetted piece of wood, with either the same or different subjects. It is also possible to inlay relief carvings, particularly very shallowly carved ones, with metal, stone, plastic or shell, or with other woods. Some peoples particularly skilled at relief carving, like the New Zealand Maori and American Northwest Coast Indians, inlay many of their carvings with shell as a matter of custom. So do some furniture makers, particularly in France.

Most modern relief carving is low relief and made in relatively small pieces exhibited at or near eye level. Low-relief carving, however, is particularly susceptible to light intensity and direction, so such work as a pediment high above eye level or a boat counter well below may require special correction. Also, the third dimension in any relief carving is not simply a flattened version of the actual or in-the-round dimension—it often must incorporate a difference in shape. A rounded surface may have to be carved somewhat angular to produce an edge that creates a difference in light reflection. A given line may have to be shorter or longer than a matching one on the opposite side of center, since elements that would normally be at different depths must be at about the same depth. Thus, differentials must be optical.

Effects must be created by texturing, by making a simple groove different on either side, by flattening or even gouging a surface and even by tinting and "antiquing" (my own word for darkening deeper lines and areas). Tinting or painting on relief carvings, however, is not done nearly as often as it is on the in-the-round figures, possibly because the latter are often the adult equivalent of toys while relief carvings are more nearly decoration.

It was the custom before and after Grinling Gibbons, master of the silhouetted and high-relief floral swag, to cover almost all of a surface with intricate patterns, usually incorporating vines and foliage in some fashion. One authority said that the English and Germans believed 50 percent or so of a surface should be carved, the Italians 80 percent or more and the Indians and Chinese 100 percent. Modern carvers tend to hold back, carving only portions of a surface and leaving the wood grain itself to show over extensive areas. In fact, there is much use of wood grain left utterly plain. Economy may be involved in some of this, just as it is in mounting a carved or uncarved silhouette against a contrasting background that may be glass, plastic or textile rather than wood.

Geometric patterns, bust portraits and floral groups are essentially in one plane, so perspective is not a problem; nor is composition, except in the case of the floral group. Thus, it is relatively easy to carve any of these in relief. But too many neophytes promptly decide to make a scene or multiple group. And therein often lies basic trouble, because creating an artistic composition or scene requires at least a little knowledge of art.

First are the basic rules for composition, which appear in any text on drawing or painting. They include these: Elements should not all be in the same pose, or of the same size; elements should not touch, but should either be clearly separate or overlap; a line or shape in a frontal element should not be immediately next to a similar line or shape in the background.

Eliminate extraneous details as scale is reduced. Look around you and you'll see that at a relatively short distance the nails in a fence and the veins in leaves disappear. At greater distance, the fence palings or rails begin to blur and the leaves themselves merge into a green tree silhouette. At a little distance, cats don't have whiskers, birds don't have feathers and men have no lines in their faces. If you put such details in, you create a sort of cartoon or caricature rather than a picture. It is also unnecessary to show every branch of a tree, every number on a license plate or house, every pane in a window or every shingle on a roof, particularly if it is back a bit in the composition. You don't have to fill every part of the picture with objects. In nature there is open sky, clear fields and smooth water—you'll find the hard way that adding waves, individual leaves and clouds is very difficult in woodcarving. *Suggest* a telephone or power line; don't try to carve the wires unless you need them to support a flock of birds. Leave out elements of the background that are unessential to the story you're trying to tell or to identification of the scene. Your eye does the same thing—you don't notice detail unless you study a scene very closely. A painter can grey or blur such elements, suggest them with a blob of color. But you cannot to the same degree, so it is often better to leave them out entirely. Even on a head portrait, it is not necessary to carve away the background all the way to the edge or to some rigid mechanical shape; the panel itself provides that. Framing, too, is often unnecessary, as an unframed carving can suggest that a scene goes beyond the limits of the wood.

Another vital consideration is perspective. Primitive painters and carvers are not concerned with it, but everybody else *is*, including the viewer. Under normal circumstances, it is unlikely that you will be considered a primitive; you are far more likely to be judged simply as crude, whether your friends tell you so or not. Remember: A nearby house is larger than its mate that is farther away, the rear of a house is smaller than the front and the far ends are smaller than the middle. You must learn about vanishing points and how to achieve the effect of distance on a flat surface just as a painter must. If you don't, your people and buildings will look like postage stamps poorly stuck against a background, and a continuous line of anything—road, people, train cars, flying birds—will look very wrong. Things in nature are not rigid and unchanging unless they're dead. There is always some variation between like objects, animate or inanimate. There is also perspective that effects size and shape; for example, an animal standing at an angle to you will appear to lose size at the farthest portion of its body.

Fig. 24. Small oak picture frame from Italy shows florid and deep-relief formal style of the past century. It combines several motifs and is made to appear even heavier with black stain.

Figs. 25–26 (above and right). In these panels by T. E. Haag of Tualatin, Oregon, a textured background clarifies the silky smoothness of the figure itself.

It is very easy to design a panel so that an object in the background looks too large compared to one nearer your eye, to attempt to put an essentially tall object in a wide frame or to have a free-form object in a rigid panel (or vice versa). There is such a thing as deliberate distortion for emphasis, but it is a weak defense for a beginner. You've got to learn first how to do it right, something many "modern artists" have never learned. One good way to incorporate perspective and composition into a carving is to take various photographs of the subject or scene and have a jury of friends pick the best one. Then you can project the negative and trace the parts you want or have an enlargement made to your intended size (if it is within reason) to serve as both a pattern and a guide. All in all, I find the polyglot panel (see those for a door in Chapter 15) much easier to plan and carve, because even scale is abandoned.

When laying out a panel, use pencil rather than pen unless the wood is dark and you are sure all lines will be cut away. I have had cleanup problems with soft-tip pen lines, particularly in color on light woods where the ink may penetrate and stain. On most panels, it is not necessary to sink the background very deeply. I have one in ebony in which the background is so shallow that it is really distinguished only by its surface pattern. Depth is, of course, a matter of choice. The deeper you go, the more modelling you can do (and the more like in-the-round carving it is); but you will also encounter proportionately more undercutting and lateral-view problems. It is easier, and much faster, to learn something about perspective and panel carving before you attempt a piece like *The Last Supper* for your church and find, when you've finished, that the minister or priest decides it will hang best in some dimly lit alcove.

On small panels, I often do not sink the background more than ⅛ in (3.2 mm); on larger pieces like my "bug tree," I may ground to a depth of ½ in (13 mm) or more. Several factors will determine a practical grounding depth—namely, how many elements are overlapping, how much detail is involved and how much modelling is necessary. If there are several planes of depth, it is best to ground a little deeper in most cases (at least until you learn how to make one object appear in front of another). Also, there is the matter of panel thickness; if it is relatively thin, say 1 in (2.54 cm) or less, it is inadvisable to ground deeply. If extensive modelling is to be done on a bust, for example, or on some other fairly complex figure, it may be advisable to ground as deeply as 1 in (2.54 cm). Also, when you ground, the difference in top and bottom surface areas may cause the panel to warp slightly during carving.

Cutting down the background, or grounding, is done this way: First, outline the area to be lowered with a V-tool or veiner. This cuts surface fibres and reduces the likelihood of splintering at the surface. Then drive in suitable gouges and firmers vertically along the notch to limit the cut area. I usually use small ones, such as ⅛ and ¼ in (3.2 and 6.4 mm) wide. If grounding is shallow, the setting-in or vertical cutting can be done in a single step, but usually it is best to take it in several steps to avoid crushing and breakage from the tool heel's wedging action. It is thus possible to set-in $\frac{1}{16}$ to ⅛ in (1.6 to 3.2 mm) per step, depending upon wood density, hardness, tendency to split and width of sections between set-in areas (a little experimenting is advisable here). After the line is set-in, cut down the area to be grounded with a flat gouge along the cut lines, then set-in deeper—and so on. Final depth can be measured with a pin gauge, a mark on a rule or scale or the like, but I find that in most cases my eye is accurate enough. This is true particularly when the background is to be textured or antiqued, in which case slight variations in depth from grounded area to grounded area are unimportant. It is also possible, if areas are relatively large and simple in outline, to rout the wood out. This assures a fairly uniform depth but may create burned lines, gouged spots and the like, as is usual with power carving.

On grounding work, I almost always use a light mallet with the chisels. It gives me better control of the tool and is less likely to cause breakouts and running of the tool into splits. Avoid wedging out chips; this causes breakouts too. Also, when grounding on two sides of a section I am extremely careful when the width of that section is ⅜ in (9.5 mm) or less on woods

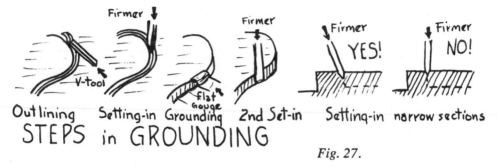

STEPS in GROUNDING

Fig. 27.

such as teak and walnut. I ground out on one side as described above, but on the other I lean the tool when setting-in so that its edge cuts into the area to be grounded and away from the narrow section. The wood remaining will then be thicker at the bottom than at the top and require a follow-up operation to make the edge vertical, but this is better than glueing back a split-out section. I find, from years of performing this operation, that larger tools can do more damage than the time they save. Large gouges, for example, will tend to break out the wood inside the sweep, which is just too bad if you are outlining a convex arc. Also, the flat gouge is a much better roughing tool than the firmer, which tends to catch at the corners and gouge additional, deeper lines. (A remedy for this problem is to grind off the corners of the firmer slightly, making what is called a bullnose tool.) When the ground is fairly level, a firmer can be used for final smoothing—if you really want it smooth. In this cleanup operation, you may also find dog-leg tools very helpful for getting into tight spots. I find that in really tight corners my penknife is still my safest tool.

After you use a mallet for a while, you will develop a rhythm of, say, two or three light taps per cut. But watch out—the same strength of blow will drive the chisel in deeper with the grain than across it. You'll find it best to ground out large areas first and then go back to do the smaller and intricate areas with more care. You should also set-in across-grain first, so any tendency to split as you set-in along the grain will be halted by a previously cut line. I find that I may work progressively, doing some grounding and then some modelling and even final carving in rotation. This relieves the boredom of setting-in for days before you can get at the interesting part. I also start at the bottom of a carving in most cases. Then my hands and arms rub in some patina and, if it's a warm day, they don't erase as-yet-uncarved lines. I find, too, that I can then feel rough spots and clean them up early, thus saving final cleanup time.

Finish or texture of the background varies with subject, relative areas of background, flat surfaces in the subject, depth of grounding and the like. Large areas of background should probably be subordinated in some way, either by texturing them to break up—rather than reflect—light rays or by antiquing them slightly with stain. In the Far East, the tendency is to texture all backgrounds with small stamps; simple ones can be produced by filing lines across the flattened end of a spike. The pattern should be small, so it does not mash major fibres and cause splintering of the ground. Another device is to break up the background by shallow veiner or V-tool lines in either a regular or random pattern. An easier but less positive method is to produce a pattern of small depressions with a relatively flat spoon gouge or a dental burr or ball cutter in a rotary tool. I find darkening the background preferable because it also makes the grounding appear deeper and accents the lines of the carving. On porous woods, such a treatment should be preceded by a couple of coats of matte varnish to seal the surface and reduce contrast between end-grain and cross-grain areas. Stain should be brushed in carefully, wiped off after a short interval, and should not be a great deal darker than the surface color. On woods like apple, I use mahogany; on teak I use walnut and on walnut I use walnut stain with a little black added. (Don't use black as a background unless you intend to be startling, because black is "dead" unless it has a shine.)

When you model the surface of a design, it is actually a repetition of grounding and should be done in much the same way, with stop cuts to prevent splitting off of surface wood. The basic difference is that the modelling will probably not be more than a third as deep as the background, unless the background is very shallow. Do *not* begin by chamfering all edges the way a whittler does a dog blank. You may want to keep some edges sharp and hard so they stand out and up. Rounding an edge in relief carving tends to obliterate or subordinate it—and you want scales, feather or hair-lines and the like to be visible. Small features like an eye or a brow line can on occasion be inverted as grooves instead of raised surfaces. And errors can sometimes be corrected simply by carving the erroneous area a little deeper and increasing the depth of the adjacent area until there is no sharp break. However, any really deep correction will be visible in most lighting.

Most ancient Greek statues had the eyes painted in, so the eye itself was rounded as it is in nature, and the figure appears to be blind. My remedy for this is to drill a small-diameter hole for the iris, which blocks out light and looks appropriately black. I mention this here because it is a kind of texturing you will find necessary if panels are to be convincing. A flat surface reflects light, even without sanding and reflective finishes. This is true particularly in hard woods if you cut with sharp tools rather than dull ones or rasps, rotary grinding burrs or other primarily abrasive wood removers. Thus, to reduce glare and highlights where you don't want them, you must texture the area. This can be done exactly as you would on the background—with a pattern or random cutting of shallow veiner or V-tool lines, or by stamping with very small and overall patterns. Any of these textures breaks up impinging light rays and reduces reflections.

A few more pointers: If your tool slips or something else goes wrong, repair the spot at once before you lose the chip or magnify the error. Use a good grade of glue with the cut-out chip, with another whittled to proper shape (be sure it's also proper in grain and color) or even with mixed glue and sawdust as a filler. Then work somewhere else for a while, admittedly a hard thing to do. I use Elmer's Glue-all® for most carvings but find a plastic cement better for outside work. Also, Elmer's works fine for appliquéing pieces of wood or building up a blank and, in such cases, can be cut 50-50 with water. It then penetrates deeper, dries faster and saves glue by covering more surface more easily. In any case, sand or cut away any glue spillage because it is likely to affect the finish later on.

If you want particular thickness only in some areas, buy wood in a thick-ness necessary for the panel and glue scraps on top in the areas that must be thicker. I've done this for a coat-of-arms on a panel, the bulge of a hull and for a special element on the front corner of a house. The same technique can be used to take care of a rotted, discolored or worm-eaten area. Just cut out the rot or knot and replace it with a selected piece of the same wood carefully fitted to the hole. It may prove better to have an irregular shape than a regular one, since masking such a line is often easier. Be sure any large filled area has the same color and grain (or figure) as the wood around it. And don't sand the area until you're done, if then—imbedded grains of sand can play havoc with the edge of a woodcarving tool.

It is also important to experiment with V-cuts or others when defining the edge of something. A V-cut that makes an accurate vee with the surface will simply be a defining line, but a V-cut with one side vertical and the other faired out onto the adjacent surface will make the edge behind the vertical wall appear to be higher than the adjacent surfaces. Cheeks can be given the appearance of being behind a nose by making the nostril lines sharply vertical and the nose outline above them more vertical than the curves of the cheeks. The same thing applies to brow and ear lines, beard lines and hairlines on faces, as well as to scenes. One panel I saw recently included three houses, each looking as if it had been pasted atop a crudely shaped mound. The problem was that the carver had a vertical V-cut along the bottom of the house so that it projected from, rather than rested on, the ground. The perspective was also wrong. These things must be learned through experimentation; you can't carve a good *Last Supper* on the first try, any more than Leonardo could paint it.

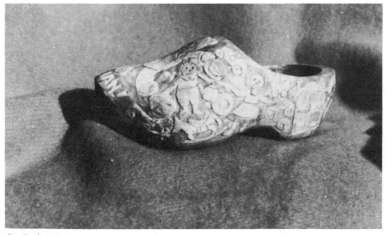

Fig. 28. Relief carving need not be on a planar surface. This is a willow-wood shoe from the Netherlands that I carved in polyglot fashion. Motifs pictured are familiar children's toys.

Figs. 29–30–31 (above and below). Araucano and Araucana (male and female) busts in mahogany-like rauli wood are modern high-relief silhouettes carved in Chile, where woodcarving is infrequent (possibly because of wood scarcity). Heads and chests are correct in the third dimension, while back halves of bodies are flattened. Each is about 6 in (15 cm) tall.

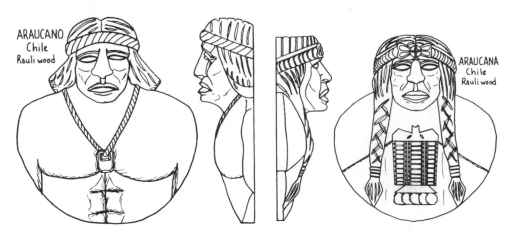

ARAUCANO
Chile
Rauli wood

ARAUCANA
Chile
Rauli wood

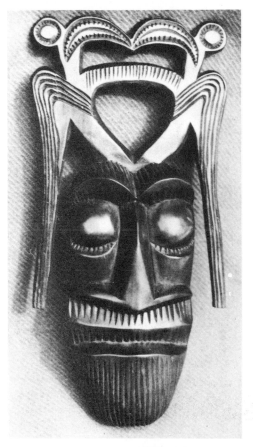

Fig. 32 (left). This "mask" from Easter Island is actually a flat panel for wall hanging. It illustrates the strength of stylized modern surfaces and shapes, incorporating pierced carving and simple V-groove texturing. It is about 14 in (36 cm) tall.

Fig. 33 (above). Russian bowl is lacquer-finished, then decorated in relief with gouge cuts through to the base wood.

Fig. 34 (below). Attenuated silhouette figures such as these from Israel are actually relief carvings—third dimension is negligible.

Figs. 35–36–37 (left, above and on facing page). These seem like in-the-round carving but are actually medium relief on the surface of a log. They are by Bogosav Zivkovic, and are now in a gallery in Svetozarevo, Yugoslavia.

Fig. 37.

Figs. 38–39 (left and below). Teak box about 4 × 6 in (10 × 15 cm) is probably from Sri Lanka; it has the familiar elephant motif on the lid and even more familiar lotus and floral designs on its sides. Backgrounds, typical of East Indian work, are stippled all over—probably with a punch—and figures are stylized to a considerable degree.

Edge of front

Edge of top panel

Elements are modelled

Hinged joint

Note that flower has 7 petals

Background stippled with punch or veiner

Lotus-petal bands on top rim

EAST INDIAN MOTIFS on a teak box

Figs. 40–41 (above and left). Two bird panels by T. E. Haag illustrate the wide range of scenic depiction possible in low relief. Figure 40 (above) shows a detailed duck against a textured background, while figure 41 (below) depicts three stylized flying swans against a patterned background. One is framed, the other has an unusual outlining with latitude and longitude lines, bowed and spaced to give the flat panel a global effect.

CHAPTER V

Belt Buckles, Plain and Fancy

Two experts share their experience with you

BELT BUCKLES ARE AN EASY, UTILITARIAN way to display both beautiful wood and good carving. Structure and design can suit your fancy, ranging from simple line patterns to elaborate modelling, appliqués or inlays of metal or stone on both exhibited front and important back ends. You can also inset small shaped pieces such as gears or animals in a plastic set into a well of wood. My childhood crony John Phillip, now of Whittier, California, and Harrison Neustadt, of Sunrise, Florida, have each made dozens of buckles for gift or sale. Mr. Neustadt has even designed jigs for bending and inserting the findings into the wood without splitting. He usually makes the buckle of wood alone, while Mr. Phillip backs the wood with a metal frame to which the findings are soldered.

The basic ingredient is an interesting piece of wood cut to a blank of the desired shape—round, oval, square, rectangular, petiolate or free form. It should be ¼ to ⅜ in (6.4 to 9.5 mm) thick and a bit wider than the standard belt widths of 1, 1½ or 2 in (2.54, 4 or 5.1 cm). If buckle length is more than about 2 in (5.1 cm), the shape should be slightly curved to fit the abdomen. If the blank is circular, it can be turned and ridged or otherwise machine-shaped before carving.

John Phillip's favorite fastening is based on a clip, or combined hook, that can be stainless steel, brass or even a coat-hanger or similar stiff iron wire. The bent form should be strong enough to resist midriff expansion after a heavy meal, so that anything attached need only support itself. The loop end (see sketches) is made to fit the desired belt width, and the hook engages in the belt holes. The belt, incidentally, is usually the kind that comes with snaps for easy buckle interchange. You can also cut an undistinguished buckle off a standard belt and rivet one of these in its place because the new assembly adds a couple of inches of length.

Least complicated is stapling the clip to the back of the blank. You can make suitable staples by bending brads into U's after sharpening both ends. The brads should not be long enough to go through the blank and in brittle or very hard wood, or in cross-grain pieces, they should be driven into pre-drilled holes. A more secure design involves routing or grooving a slot of the desired shape into the wood, then glueing the clip in securely. However, Mr. Phillip usually solders the clip onto a plate of thin stainless, brass or copper of the blank shape and contour, roughens the face of the backing and glues on the wood. The backing plate should not be more than $\frac{1}{16}$ in (1.6 mm) thick or the buckle will be overweight. You can use a very thin plate and leave it sufficiently oversize to crimp it around the wood as a jeweller sets a gem into a bezel, but this is normally unnecessary because there is little stress on the facing.

Mr. Neustadt uses no backing. His findings are just the C-shaped clip and a pin, both forced by a jig into pre-drilled holes. The findings have grooves near the ends, so glue will hold them in place.

Finish can suit your taste. I usually use a spray coat or two of matte varnish, followed by waxing. Mr. Neustadt has been using his own mixture for 20 years on all of his craftwork, including furniture, bowls and platters. It is a 50-50 mixture of polyurethane and boiled linseed oil, applied with an old sock. He says that his earliest pieces have improved with age and now have a lovely patina.

If you want to inlay metal or stone inserts in the face of the buckle, set them securely so they do not catch clothing. Mr. Phillip does it by placing the insert where he wants it, clamping it, then scratching around it with a sharp scriber. He reinforces the scribed line with a series of sharp center-punch holes, then routs the socket in his drill press with a small bit running at high speed. In this way he can shape areas that a knife would chip and break out. He drills only as deep as the insert, of course. The cavity is filled with Goodyear Pliobond® cement, enough so that the adhesive will seep out around the edges when the insert is seated. Next, he sprinkles fine-sanding dust from the wood (be sure it is the same wood) all around the edge and mixes it with the adhesive. Then he taps the insert all over with a small mallet—or hammer, if it is metal—to fill any gaps or small breakouts. He folds a small piece of waxed paper over the glued assembly to prevent sticking, on top of which is laid a block of hard wood, sawed to the same radius as the buckle top, with a gap to clear any projecting surface. He then sets three small clamps at ends and center and allows at least 48 hours drying time. When the assembly is dry, he removes block and paper, sands and fine-files the surface, then paraffin-buffs.

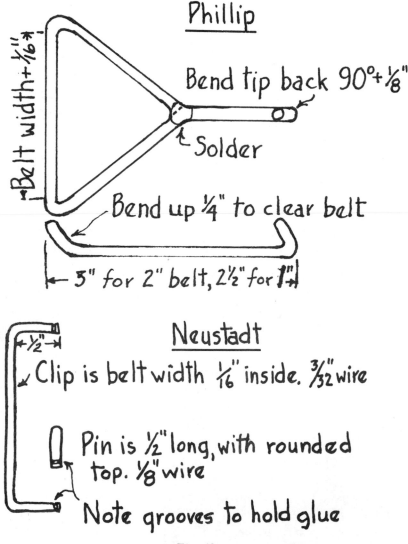

Phillip

Belt width + ⅟₁₆"

Bend tip back 90°+ ⅛"

Solder

Bend up ¼" to clear belt

← 3" for 2" belt, 2½" for 1" →

Neustadt

←½"→

Clip is belt width ⅟₁₆" inside. ³⁄₃₂" wire

Pin is ½" long, with rounded top. ⅛" wire

Note grooves to hold glue

Fig. 42.

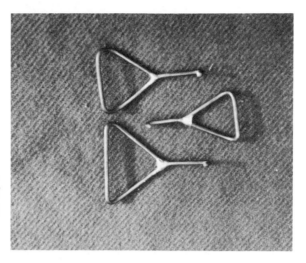

Fig. 43. John Phillip's form-ed clips to fit 1-, 1½- and 2-in (2.54-, 3.8- and 5-cm) belts. Joints are soldered.

Fig. 44. Top buckle is 1¾ × 3¾ in (4.4 × 9.6 cm), curved, of South American walnut relief-carved with a buck's head. Upper-left buckle is redwood burl 1¾ × 2½ in (4.4 × 6.4 cm), with chamfering only. One at upper right is California walnut burl, 2¼ × 3 in (5.7 × 7.6 cm), with inlaid masks of walrus ivory, hand-carved in relief. At lower left is Australian gum, turned and carved to fit a lady's 1-in (2.54-cm) belt. Lower right buckle is California walnut, 2¼ × 3 in (5.7 × 7.6 cm), with Indian sun design of darkened grooves and gold-stone insert.

41

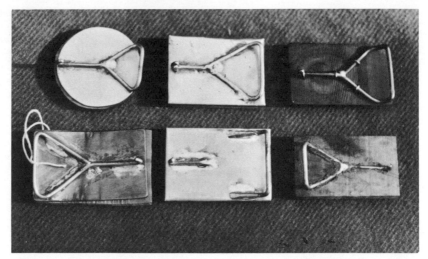

Fig. 45. Varied buckle-back arrangements by John Phillip include soldered clips on stainless (top left) and brass (lower left). At upper right is a clip secured with staples made of 1-in (2.54-cm) bent brads. At lower right, the clip has been glued into a groove. (Neither of these has a backing of metal.) At top center is a two-part clip, while at bottom center the backing of thin stainless has been crimped like a bezel around the wood front. Here, a separate pin and clip are soldered to the backing.

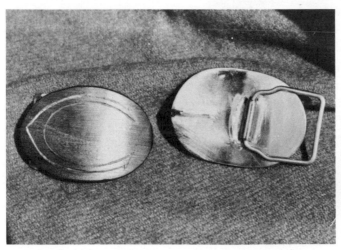

Fig. 46. A more elaborate clip, hinged in a soldered-on socket to give greater flexibility. The pin is soldered on separately. Face is walnut, incised with a simple initial.

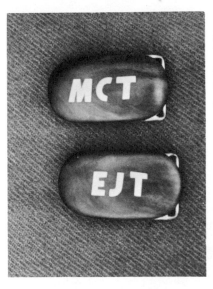

Fig. 47 (left). "His" and "Hers" matching buckles of walnut, curved, with inlaid stainless initials. By John Phillip.

Fig. 48. This walnut facing is carved with a trenched low-relief prairie dog I copied from a photograph.

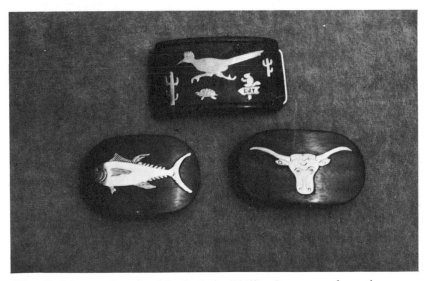

Fig. 49. More walnut buckles by John Phillip. Inserts are brass for upper one and steer head, stainless for fish.

CHAPTER VI

Crystal Gazer—A Composite

PERIODICALLY, I FIND IT INTERESTING to make a composite carving, combining wood with some other object or material to provide a striking contrast. Thus, I have used a gold wedding ring to make a king's crown, an actual fishing fly caught in a trout's jaw, real chain or cord and so on. The idea is merely a variation of the familiar inlaying with shell, metal or other woods for contrast. In this particular example, however, my intention was to provide some form of display mounting for a 4-in (10-cm) crystal ball I have owned for over 40 years.

The original thought was merely to carve a pedestal covered with cabalistic symbols, primarily a pillar with the ball at the top. It seemed more interesting, however, to carve a gypsy woman with the ball, so that the crystal-gazing concept would be emphasized. The objective was to feature the ball and allow it to catch the maximum amount of light. Any frontal panel seemed to enclose it too much, as did any composition in which the hands of the figure hovered over it. My ultimate choice was a side view with the ball cupped in the gypsy's hands, the entire figure of the gypsy thus becoming a silhouette and a support for the ball (Fig. 50). This effect was accentuated by the decision not to detail the figure and, further, to cover it with a scalloped texture produced with a relatively flat ¾-in (19-mm) gouge. I had a block of well seasoned maple 4¼ × 16½ × 16½ in (11 × 42 × 42 cm).

The final design was simply drawn on the block and sawed out on a bandsaw. Figures 51 to 55 explain the steps. The figure can be readily adapted to hold something else, of course. On a half-size carved later in mahogany, wood thickness permitted wider shoulders and elbows, hence more natural proportions and greater stability in the figure.

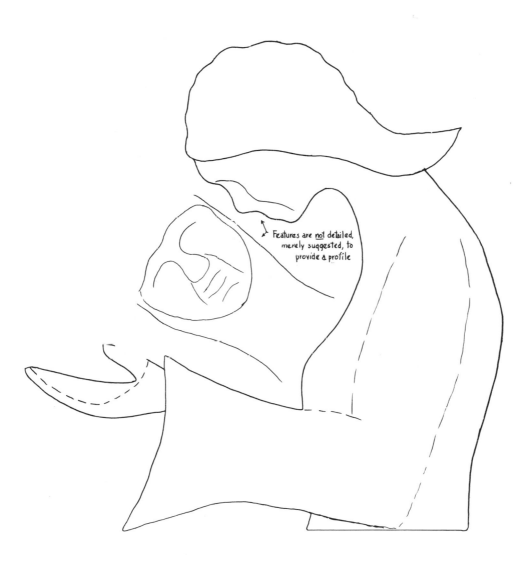

Features are <u>not</u> detailed,
merely suggested, to
provide a profile

Fig. 50. Crystal Gazer is maple, 4½ × 16½ × 16½ in (10 × 42 × 42 cm). It was designed to feature a 4-in (10-cm) crystal ball, and is largely a silhouette with scallop-textured surfaces.

Fig. 51. Stylized gypsy seer was carved almost entirely with ¾-in (19-mm) No. 6 gouge and finished with wax only. A later commission (foreground) included a 1¾-in (4.4-cm) Christmas-tree ball.

Fig. 52. Block is laid out with a soft-tipped pen by eye. It is then sawed out in a bandsaw. Grain is horizontal for strength in hands and ease when scalloping.

Fig. 53 (above). First cuts are made to rough-shape the figure and define hairline. Hands are hollowed and shaped early so ball can be checked in position as carving progresses. Fig. 54 (below). After rough-shaping, face is defined with simple lines that establish nose, eye and cheek, though no details are put in beyond eyebrow line. Hands are thinned and shaped, but fingers are not defined yet either.

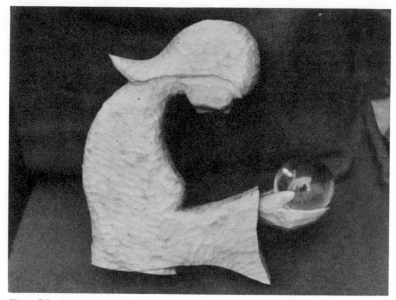

Fig. 55. Because of horizontal grain, scalloping with the gouge is relatively easy. Scallop lines are with grain whenever possible. Nose bridge is thinned and chin rounded; hairline is sharpened with a ¼-in (6.4-mm) No. 8 or 9 gouge—also helpful in shaping the face.

Fig. 56. Doubling width of the smaller version permitted wider shoulders and elbows, thus normalizing proportions. It also resulted in greater stability, since thickness is proportional to height.

Fig. 57 (above). Half-inch (13-mm) slabs cut from sides of smaller blank permitted this exercise in head styling—something that should never be missed—as well as that pictured below. At right, head silhouette is stylized with rough-sawed surface left on bandanna for texture, while at left face has been formed and knot added to bandanna. Fig. 58 (below). Rough-shaped head at left is more defined here, with eyes, nose and mouth positioned and bandanna smooth. At right, face is fully formed, ear defined, and hair slightly textured and held by a barrette.

CHAPTER VII

Northwest Coast Carving Designs

The totem pole is only one example of a "different" style

SOME PEOPLES AND TRIBES are inherent craftsmen, others are not, and this seems to have little to do with their intelligence. To some degree, differences in terrain, day-to-day needs and available materials are all influences, as are creativity and sense of design. Among American Indians, the Northwest Coast tribes of Southern Alaska and British Columbia have been outstanding for their work in wood. The Eskimos of both coasts worked ivory and bone to a limited degree, as well as soft stone; but the Indian tribes of the Northwest Coast developed a much wider range of subjects and a greater sense of decoration and symbolism, of which the totem pole is a relatively recent example. Much older and less well-known are oil or grease bowls, spoons (many of mountain-sheep horn), various tools, weapons and the decorated council houses. The old arts are dying out there as elsewhere and much of what is currently available is corrupted for the tourist trade. But the work is still distinctive and interesting and includes a number of ideas readily adaptable by other carvers.

The pieces illustrated and sketched here include both traditional and more modern designs, with relatively little attention to the totem pole, which is a somewhat specialized art incorporating familial and religious elements. The word totem pole, incidentally, is a specific thing, not a general term for any vertical carved pole—particularly surface-carved ones.

Woods commonly carved in the Northwest are cedar and pine; much of the work is painted. Some pieces have inserts of abalone shell, apparently for decoration alone rather than having the significance of the somewhat

Fig. 59. Standard totem pole is a series of in-the-round animals one atop another—like this one in a Vancouver, British Columbia, park. Some, however, may be high relief with no back carving (note that this one is backed by a pine tree).

similar paua-shell inserts in Maori carving. Figures are stylized, many of them mythical or religious, and are often grouped to recall a legend or imply a force or power. Many surface-decoration patterns are incorporated, the carving done with bold strokes and relatively deep incising. Many of the old totem poles were carved with a hard stone axe (and show it), and smaller work and detail were done with the D-adze or with a triangular-bladed knife.

It is possible to miniaturize many of the designs. I have included two miniature totem poles (Figs. 62 and 63), two oil or grease bowls (Figs. 67 and 69), several charms or pendants, and a number of the Indian motifs in sketch form (Figs. 70 and 72). The shaman's mask (Fig. 61) is my own. Additional designs may be found in many books; one of the best is the analysis by Bill Holm, *Northwest Coast Indian Art*, published by the University of Washington Press. Prices in the area for elaborate pieces are extremely high—another excellent reason for making your own.

Eskimo and Indian craftsmen of today use power drills, chain saws, files and sandpaper, instead of their traditional tools, and most of their production is geared for tourists. Even so, some pieces are made on machines in cities such as Seattle, then shipped to the area; others are produced in the Philippines, Japan or wherever prices are lower. The brown bear with a salmon—a traditional Alaskan piece—is now carved by the Ainu in Japan.

The primary thing in making any of these pieces is to be bold in your cuts and sparing with the sandpaper, which blurs sharp lines. Basswood, pine and cedar are suitable woods because the pieces will probably be painted anyway. Flat designs are occasionally done in colors, and I have indicated such variations on some of the designs by shading. Miniatures, however, can simply be flat carvings with the background sunk rather deeply in proportion —this makes the carving stand out in bold relief. Some of the designs are quite complex, and are modern variations of old designs that, through the years, have become increasingly abstract and symbolic.

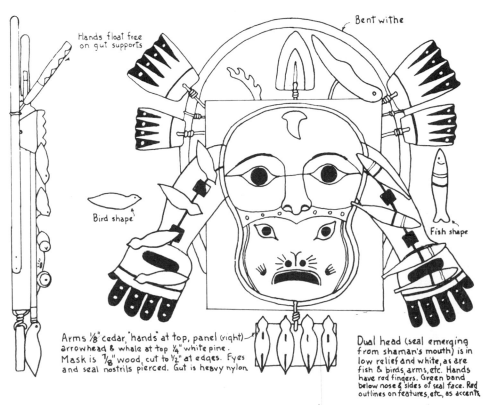

Hands float free on gut supports

Bent withe

Bird shape

Fish shape

Arms ⅛" cedar, "hands" at top, panel (right) arrowhead & whale at top ¼" white pine. Mask is ⅞" wood, cut to ½" at edges. Eyes and seal nostrils pierced. Gut is heavy nylon.

Dual head (seal emerging from shaman's mouth) is in low relief and white, as are fish & birds, arms, etc. Hands have red fingers. Green band below nose & sides of seal face. Red outlines on features, etc., as accents.

SHAMAN'S DANCE MASK (Alaska)
Late 19th Century. Painted: green, red & white

Figs. 60–61 (above and left). I made this tinted miniature of a shaman's dance mask from the late 19th century. The original was so elaborate that it was probably carried rather than worn. It depicted animals and was used to assure success in the hunt.

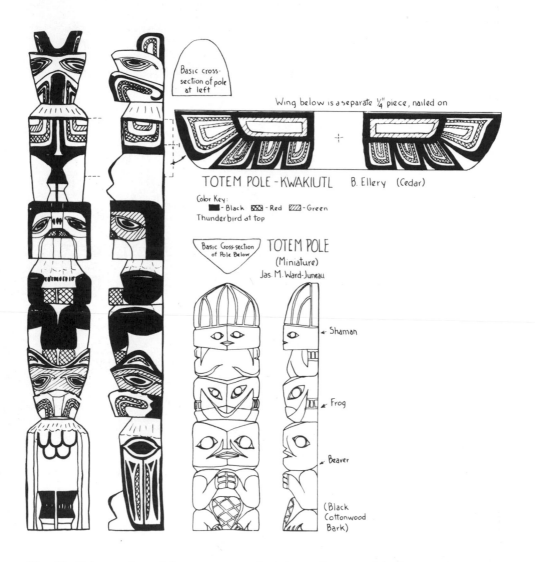

Basic cross-section of pole at left

Wing below is a separate ¼" piece, nailed on

TOTEM POLE - KWAKIUTL   B. Ellery   (Cedar)

Color Key:
■ - Black   ▨ - Red   ▨ - Green
Thunderbird at top

Basic Cross-section of Pole Below

TOTEM POLE
(Miniature)
Jas. M. Ward - Juneau

← Shaman

← Frog

← Beaver

(Black Cottonwood Bark)

Fig. 62. Patterns for miniature totem poles pictured at top of facing page.

Fig. 63. Miniature totem poles such as these are primarily tourist items, though they may be faithful copies. The one at left is about 12 in (30 cm) tall and painted, and shows two birds sandwiching a human figure. Totem pole at right is about 6 in (15 cm) tall and unpainted, and is a shaman atop a frog atop a beaver; it is particularly interesting because it is carved in black cottonwood bark rather than the usual cedar.

Figs. 64–65 (above and left). A traditional Northwest Indian carving is this black bear with a salmon. They are now imported from Japan and made there by the Ainu for less than they could be in Alaska. Design can be either in-the-round or relief.

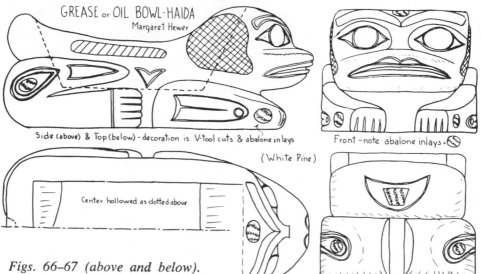

GREASE or OIL BOWL-HAIDA
Margaret Hewer

Side (above) & Top (below) - decoration is V-tool cuts & abalone inlays

(White Pine)

Center hollowed as dotted above

Front - note abalone inlays =

Rear - three abalone inserts

Figs. 66–67 (above and below). The Haida were noted for carvings with abalone inserts. This modern one, by an Indian woman, is about a foot (30 cm) long and is an oil or grease bowl—in which a wick burning in whale oil provides a house with light and some heat.

OIL BOWL-TLINGIT

Cross-section
from below head
(Cedar)

(Miniature)

J.O. Rowan-Ketch.

Center hollow

Figs. 68–69 (above and below). This miniature of a Tlingit oil bowl was made by J. O. Rowan of Ketchikan, Alaska. It is a sea otter on its back, with paint spots replacing the shell inserts used on full-sized carvings. Stylizing makes it practically a shaped panel.

WASGO or MONSTER

Can be panel or in-the-round figure

Fig. 70.

DOG

Indian motifs and charms.

Fig. 72.

DOLPHIN or KILLER WHALE

Fig. 71. Polar bear

Seal

CHARMS

Eskimo or Indian
(Black Cottonwood Bark)
Shown actual size

CHAPTER VIII

Carving a Cameo

IF YOU HAVE A PIECE OF WOOD WITH STRONG CONTRAST between strata, or between heart wood and growth wood, it is possible to get a special effect—that of a cameo such as is carved in multilayered shell—by having the figure in one color of wood against the background of the other. Woods like walnut and apple can provide such a contrast, and a number of foreign woods can provide very strong contrasts, if that is desired.

The subject can be a mammal or a bird, or even a scene. An interesting added effect is obtained if the carving is made in a section of log, with or without the bark. As an example, I used a green section of apple, complete with bark, selected from a pile I was splitting for firewood. The blank was roughly triangular in cross-section, about 4 in (10 cm) deep by 6 in (15 cm) wide by 18 in (46 cm) long.

My design was a Nereid (water fairy) that followed the curvature of the log, with hands and feet disappearing into the ends of the block, and the background cut away to expose the growth wood. Because of the particular twisted pose, the figure is practically in the round. Carving followed the conventional cycle of setting-in, grounding out, then modelling, all of the heavy work being done with relatively flat gouges and firmers in the ¼- to ½-in (6.4- to 13-mm) range, with details carved by knife. There was no detailing of the face or hair, and the sides were left somewhat rough.

Carving wood while it is green is easier than carving it when it is dry, but here it was necessary to give the finished carving several coats of matte varnish, particularly on the ends, to avoid or reduce checking during drying. It may also be necessary to touch up the back of the figure with stain to accentuate the contrast and emphasize the shape without extensive under-cutting.

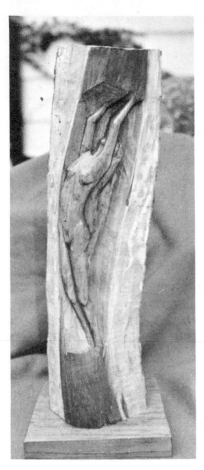

Figs. 73–74. Nereid (water fairy) follows the curvature of the log. Effect is similar to that of appliquéing a figure on a contrasting background, except that the carving is integral and less contrived in appearance.

NUDE
Apple 16" on 24" pc.
Medium to high
relief

CHAPTER IX

Variations on a Bird Theme

How the carver makes a design his own

YEARS AGO, I WAS FASCINATED BY THE STUDY of gravestone rubbings that showed how a skilled itinerant stone carver had gone from town to town westward from New England. His designs and techniques were readily recognizable from those of both his contemporaries and his imitators. The same thing is true of familiar woodcarving designs; they may be "standard" but, unless they are turned out on a duplicator, there will be slight but identifiable variations piece to piece. This is true whether it is all the work of one carver or that of several in turn. I have seen copies of my designs that are better than my originals because the carver has more skill or took more pains. I have also seen copies that are so painstaking that they have somehow lost verve and fire. I have made copies of Oberammergau splinter angels and similar work, and mine were not as strong as the originals because the German carver made strong cuts with single strokes while I whittled little chips to make sure I copied precisely. Making a given design over and over again should obviously lead to improvement, but sometimes it leads only to change because the individual is not capable of further improvement or becomes bored with the repetition.

To illustrate facets of this question, I have selected two groups of designs (Figs. 75 and 76), one with Indian variations on a bird profile, the other showing variations in the design of an American eagle for the top or splat of a wooden clock-case.

The bird designs are symbolic, and don't to my knowledge attempt to depict any particular species. They are shown in a 1916 book, *Evolution of the Bird in Decorative Art*, by Kenneth M. Chapman; all are suitable for incising, inlaying, or similar applications. They show how far stylizing can stray from the near-exact reproduction of the decoy-carver.

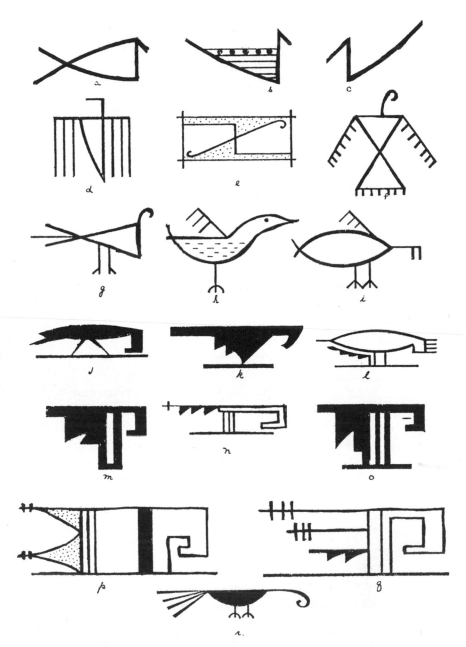

Fig. 75. Symbolic bird variations—American Indian.

1 Chauncey Ives 30-hr long case. Rare

2 G & E Bartholomew 30-hr long-pendulum

3 Riley Whiting #2 (Note differences)

4 Marsh-Gilbert 8-day.

5 Ely Terry & Son 8-day.   S. B. Terry

6 Rare

7 Silas Hoadley 30-hr. Note shield

8 Universal Eagle- many 30-hr clocks

9 Hopkins & Alfred   Rare

10 Putnam Bailey - One of a kind?

Fig. 76. Variety of American eagles.

The second group of sketches depicts research by Sheldon Hoch of White Plains, New York. He has carved mahogany copies of these eagles from his own or others' photographs of the originals. These were shown in the *Bulletin* of the National Association of Watch & Clock Collectors (Feb., '81, pp. 20–9) in which Mr. Hoch explained his project of "Hunting for Birds and Beasts in Connecticut Shelf Clocks." They are all from the American Empire period, running through Andrew Jackson's presidency (1829–37). Most clocks of that period had wooden Terry-type movements and hand-carved cases with splats depicting eagles, acanthus leaves, pineapples, paws and varied birds and beasts. Such clocks were turned out by the hundreds by a number of makers using duplicating machinery for the works, and sold for about $8. You can imagine how much the carver got for a splat; it behooved him to cut corners and work fast. None ever took time to sign his name.

First designs of this period were apparently baskets of fruit and horns of plenty (cornucopias), which were on short-case clocks. Eagles came later, usually on long-case clocks, and were more prevalent on eight-day wood-movement and 30-hour long-pendulum clocks. Each maker had his own design, almost a trademark, probably made by one or two carvers. One or two makers had more than one design, and some occasionally had unique ones. As wood-movement clocks lost out to brass-movement ones, makers like E. Terry, Jr. and Boardman & Wells went to increasingly unique, often one-of-a-kind casings with splats to match, featuring coats of arms, stylized birds and beasts or what-have-you (sometimes to order).

There are relatively few left-facing eagles. (I seem to recall that left-facing was thought to be unpatriotic by some purists.) Right-facing ones are essentially alike, suggesting a common ancestor or source design. In fact, some of the carving conventions, for feathers to name one, are repeated. Some designs have crests, others do not.

Captions with sketches identify makers. Note that both Terry designs (5 and 6) use the scroll, and that Silas Hoadley reinforced the patriotic motif with a shield (7); this design also had "The Union Be Preserved" carved on the case. Only two birds have feet (9 and 10), and were carved by the same Connecticut man for a New York company.

CHAPTER X

The Maori—Masters of Low Relief

Some of the motifs developed in a special style

IN CONTRAST TO MANY PEOPLES WHO DEVELOPED the carving of three-dimensional figures, the Maori became particularly adept at relief carving and developed a distinctive and elaborate style. Like all Polynesians, they were highly design-minded and deeply religious, and their work reflects that as well as their isolation in far off New Zealand. In contrast to many peoples in remote locations, their work actually improved for a time after the white man came, because he provided them with steel tools to replace their greenstone ones, developing a greater crispness and cleanness.

The Maori are thought to have come from Tahiti in three great migrations, the first in the 10th century and the last about 1350. The white man came in the 16th century, when their work was at its peak. By the 18th century, the Maori had become Christian, had abandoned their own gods and with them the depictions that had made their work so strong. Thereafter, the carvings became more rococo and less original, and by the 19th century, carving had already disappeared in some areas.

There is little question that some of the Maori legends about the development of carving contain elements of truth. One is that Rauru, son of Toi-kai-rakau—meaning "carver of wood" or, literally, "eater of wood"—came with his father in about 1150 and settled in Whakatane, where he developed the distinctive Maori style as opposed to his father's Tahitian or Marquesan style. This was taken up by other carvers, who had plenty to do because the climate caused rapid deterioration of most carving, and also because the house and possessions of a dead man were considered taboo, so left to rot. Much of the carving was panel work, considered sacred, and used on houses and canoes.

The carver had priestly rank and was considered gifted by the gods. He washed his hands before and after carving, begged the pardon of the trees he cut, believed his work area was contaminated by the presence of women, fire or cooked food and never blew chips away because he considered that sacrilegious!

Maori carving is different in that it features spirals, particularly 2-, 3- and even 4-way ones, usually enhanced by paua-shell inlay. Panels are often pierced and double-sided, as on a canoe prow or the outer end of a barge board (a decorative facing from ridgepole down below the eaves). In-the-round figures were limited to such uses as peak ornaments on roof fronts (the roof beams were considered ribs of the head at the peak) and on the bases of house support posts and pillars. Much of the carving was designed around the human figure, although the figure tended to be a stump type with folded and undersized legs, a rounded belly and three-fingered hands. Fish, birds, lizards, dogs and rats, plus a few legendary concoctions, were auxiliary motifs (no larger animals existed there at that time). Exposed tongues, along with spirals in the carvings at body joints and on cheeks and foreheads signifying tattoos, reflect Maori ideals and customs. To the Maori, a grimacing, tattooed male face with protruding tongue, dilated eyes and defiant hands was the essence of strength and virility.

The most highly carved building was the *pataka*, an elevated storehouse set on posts, often with bargeboards and threshold across the front incorporating pierced and shell-inlaid carving as well as carved pillars. The council houses (*whare whakairo*), which doubled as sacred buildings and residences for distinguished visitors, also contained much interior carving of posts and beams. Painting was common, the favorite wood totora—which in recent years has become so scarce that old canoes have been cut up to provide carving wood. Some of the characteristics discussed here are shown in the sketches, which also suggest the extreme elaborateness and detail of the stylized designs. There was almost no realistic carving or attempts at portraiture, though ancestor worship was tremendous.

Fig. 77. Panel in pine by Austin Brasell shows motifs that are usually background or secondary to a principal figure depicting an ancestor. White spots are paua shell; size is ¾ × 15¾ × 15¾ in (1.9 × 40 × 40 cm).

Fig. 78 (below). Typical Maori motifs.

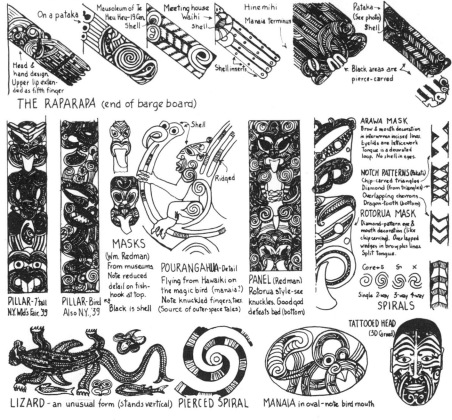

On a pataka

Mausoleum of Te Heu Heu -19 Cen. Shell

Meeting house Waihi Shell

Hine mihi Manaia terminus

Pataka (See photo) Shell

Head & hand design Upper lip extended as fifth finger

Shell inserts

Black areas are pierce-carved

THE RAPARAPA (end of barge board)

Shell

Ridged

MASKS
(Wm. Redman)
From museums
Note reduced detail on fish-hook at top.
Black is shell

POURANGAHUA-Detail
Flying from Hawaiki on the magic bird (manaia?) Note knuckled fingers, toes. (Source of outer-space tales)

PANEL (Redman)
Rotorua style-see knuckles. Good god defeats bad (bottom)

PILLAR-7'tall
N.Y. Wld's Fair.'39

PILLAR-Bird
Also N.Y.,'39

ARAWA MASK
Brow & mouth decoration is interwoven incised lines. Eyelids are latticework. Tongue is a decorated loop. No shell in eyes.

NOTCH PATTERNS (Pakati)
Chip-carved triangles
Diamond (from triangles)
Overlapping chevrons
Dragon-tooth (bottom)

ROTORUA MASK
Diamond-pattern eye & mouth decoration (like chip carving). Over lapped wedges in brow plus lines. Split tongue.

Core+S   S+   X
Single 2-way 3-way 4-way
SPIRALS

TATTOOED HEAD
(3D Carved)

LIZARD - an unusual form (stands vertical)   PIERCED SPIRAL   MANAIA in oval - note bird mouth

CHAPTER XI

Try Far Eastern Panels

Sri Lanka, India, Nepal, Tibet and Kashmir have carved for centuries

INDIA, SRI LANKA, KASHMIR, NEPAL AND TIBET all have a tradition of wood-carving that spans centuries. What survives from the old days is very competent and ornate, and is usually religious in tone. The modern work is turned out largely in "factories" for the tourist trade, and the carvers are *not* hobbyists nor artists but craftsmen earning a living. In most instances, there is one artist-designer and several carvers, often in shops with practically none of the amenities such as power saws, grinders or even electric power and light. The factory is primarily a place to work and a sales outlet. Tools, too, are limited in number; many are homemade strictly for the particular work a carver does. There may be an antique vise or two, and nothing but the floor for a bench, but there are also helpers to do preparation, sanding, finishing, polishing and other onerous chores.

In contrast to the United States, where a high percentage of carving is in-the-round and small enough to be held in the hand for whittling, many of the carvings made in this area are in relief. This ranges from very shallow, as in the case of the queen in ebony (Figs. 86 and 87), to quite-high-relief copies of old work (particularly in India, where some copies are claimed to be antique fragments). What's more, the variety is marked; carvings may be framed or unframed, geometric shapes, free-forms or silhouettes, non-planar or pierced work, in a bewildering variety of woods. Carving is of good quality, as are designs, and although it may also have pieces from other factories for sale, a particular factory is likely to be specialized. Thus, in Sri Lanka, panels are carved in the Kandy area, ebony 3-D figures in Galle, masks of *nux vomica* in one particular south-coast

Fig. 79. A carver works on a mask of nux vomica (a wood like balsa, with poisonous berries used in medicines) in a factory in Sri Lanka, while his partner tests the edge on his chisel. Carvers are pieceworkers, with nothing beyond a circular saw, flat table and bench and a tool or two apiece.

village, and so on. I could have traded a pocketknife in any factory for a really good carving; one carving school up a dirt road outside Sigiryia, Sri Lanka, had a cheap set of six American tools kept carefully in its original cardboard box. This school had no power, so used gas-pressure lamps at night for its 15 or so apprentices, who were schoolboys aged 12 to 20, who went to school in the morning and then came to apprentice in afternoons and evenings for eight long years. They should be good!

There are many varieties of wood in these countries, and factory managers are quite conversant with them; one Nepalese manager had an exhibit of woods for potential quantity buyers of carvings. Each was labelled with its correct Latin name. Ebony still seems to be available, although expensive—relatively. Most carvings are made in hard woods, so the mallet—often just a carved club—is as common as chisels. Sandalwood carvings are expensive and limited to India. One figure, the Zogini, is in a wood listed as adinacopifolia, and is carved in one piece despite elaborate projections. Pieces tend to be finished in low matte or satin, and high gloss is reserved for furniture—something Western carvers have not yet learned.

The variety in shape, technique and treatment is quite wide in these examples, which is relatively rare in areas where carving was developed later than it was here. It is interesting to me that Kashmir and Tibet both tend to carve a variety of walnut, while Nepal, India and Sri Lanka have much more variety in woods. Yet Tibet and Nepal are alike in that the population is heavily Oriental; indeed, there are 10,000 Tibetan refugees in Nepal, itself a small country. Sri Lanka, with 10 percent of the population Tamil—or recent Indian—plus tens of thousands of southern Indians as "temporary laborers" in the tea country, proclaims that it is Sinhalese (although its population is apparently Indian in origin as well). Sri Lanka is very Buddhist, India is not and so on. This affects the kinds of carvings that predominate in each country, as the pictured examples show. And it also suggests, once again, the tremendous variety available.

Fig. 80. This Nepalese scene is in sisso, an antiqued light wood, and depicts village and city with adjacent countryside. Dominant is a stupa (temple) with "paper" prayer streamers from its peak, surrounded by typical multi-storey brick and stucco buildings. Stylized rural area in foreground and at left includes rice paddies. Size is ⅞ × 6½ × 11 in (2.2 × 17 × 28 cm).

Figs. 81–82–83 (above, right and below). From far-off Tibet comes this octagonal triple folding tray in walnut. The 7-in (18-cm) sides fold down (below) to reveal carved-tray inner surfaces, plus a tilting tray in the middle. Motifs are floral.

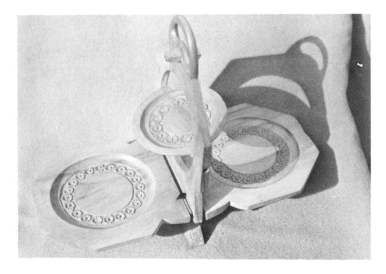

Fig. 84. All carvings are not traditional. Here are modern treatments of a praying girl in ebony ½ × 4½ × 15 in (1.3 × 10 × 38 cm) each. They were carved in Sri Lanka, and have a minimum of modelling and decoration—quite unusual there.

Fig. 85. Krishna and Raddha (Hindu god and consort) are depicted here in fret-sawed bamboo. Parts are carefully cut and glued to a backing, and some are even broken at proper points to flatten the natural curve of the stem and heighten the three-dimensional effect. Figures are about 12 in (30 cm) tall; from Sri Lanka.

Figs. 86–87 (above and right). Contrast in subject and wood is shown in these two panels. Above is a low-relief ancient queen in ebony 2¾ × 4 in (7 × 10 cm); below, a cheepu or demon head and hands in a relatively soft wood, stained black—a 7-in (18-cm) pierced carving.

Fig. 88. A panel like this delights Sri Lankans—and me. It is 6½ × 12 in (17 × 30 cm) and combines a bullock and an elephant, face to face to a greater degree than expected because they share a face and an eye.

Figs. 89–90–91. *The lotus has deep religious significance to Hindus and Buddhists alike, and is a frequent design motif. Here are an 8-in (20-cm) disk and a 5¼ × 8-in (13 × 20-cm) panel (below) from Sri Lanka that feature this design.*

Fig. 92 (right). Moonstone is familiar as the base step to Buddhist temples, and depicts the seven steps to Nirvana. In stone, it is usually a half-circle. This one, in wood, is a complete circle 14 in (36 cm) in diameter, but shows only five steps—it lacks a ring of sacred geese and another floral ring. Carving is excellent and crisp, particularly on the animals.

Fig. 93. Head-size mask of nux vomica is by Ariyapala, the best of Sri Lankan mask carvers, and is the most elaborate. Called Maha Kola Sanni, it incorporates 18 smaller masks, each a specific for curing a particular ailment in ritual healing dances. Masks cure boils, arthritis, fever and even nervousness.

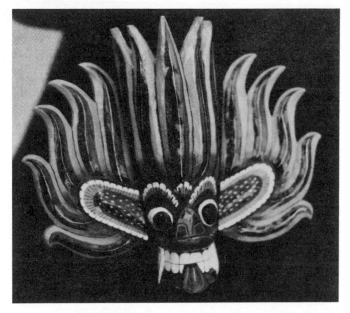

Fig. 94. Another head-size mask, depicting the fire demon featured in Kandy dances. A mask such as this takes about a week to complete, including carving and elaborate enamelling. Side projections are removable and plugged into the semi-cylinder face.

Fig. 95. Indians are masters of horn carving. Here are four examples—lion, goose, horse and pigeon—all basically relief because third dimension is flattened.

Figs. 96–97. Another delight to Sri Lankans is this variation of the Chinese puzzle box, with elephant and lotus-blossom border on its cover. It looks like a 6 × 9-in (15 × 23-cm) light-colored book, but then backbone is pushed down and back, allowing central panel to slide to the side, revealing the ¾-in (19-mm) "secret compartment."

BOX COVER
"Secret" panel in mahogany
book-shaped puzzle. Sri Lanka

Fig. 98. Unusual panel in a walnut-like wood includes growth wood and depicts three demons. It is a sort of caricature, unusual in Sri Lanka, and is 4 × 8 in (10 × 20 cm).

77

CHAPTER XII

Memories of Lebanon

Various scenes are combined in a cherry panel

GEBEL, OR JBEIL, IS IN LEBANON; it was Byblos (from which we get the word *bible*), oldest town in the world, and has been inhabited for at least 7,000 years. This cherry panel, ¾ × 7½ × 22½ in (1.9 × 19 × 57 cm), a retirement present for a Marine officer who served in Beirut some years ago, illustrates a number of basic principles of relief carving.

Fig. 99.

- The scene incorporates elements from many sources, including postals, transparencies and travel folders. The terracing at right is a composite of four sources, while the village at left is five. Some elements are introduced from elsewhere, such as Sparrow Castle, at upper right, and Pigeon Rocks, at bottom center.

- Point of view is offshore and above, so roofs can be seen on nearby buildings, giving them a third dimension. Distant structures such as the castles loom over the scene, suggesting the rise of ground. Bottoms of walls of foreground buildings and pillars are sloped backward to meet the ground. Perspective is adjusted to suit location from a higher elevation since most available photos were taken from ground level and incorporate little distance.

- The knot and knothole in the board were incorporated in the scene—one as a ruin, the other as a mountain. The knot and the graining dictated selection of this particular board for the scene.

- Relief is shallow in this case, not much over $1/8$ in (3.2 mm) in the foreground; thus, depth is enhanced by antiquing. Relief depth is greater in the foreground to suggest the haziness and blurring that occurs with distance.

- Number of elements is not too great, and detail surrounding each is reduced so that each stands out. This is decided partially by size and wood. There are few indications of brush and trees and there are no people. These clutter up the picture and are very difficult to carve realistically to scale. Texturing suggests terrain characteristics, and does not compete with elements.

CHAPTER XIII

I Sing Behind What Plough?

The saga of a symbolic panel

THIS PANEL EXEMPLIFIES SOME OF THE PROBLEMS you may face if you attempt a commemorative relief. It is in walnut, $1\frac{1}{2} \times 24 \times 36$ in ($3.8 \times 61 \times 91$ cm). The John C. Campbell Folk School, Brasstown, North Carolina, has used this symbol for most of its 55 years, but solely as a silhouette with the caption, "I sing behind the plough." The story is that the silhouette was drawn from a photo that is no longer available, and the slogan was taken from a Danish folk song by Mads Hansen, written in 1866.

I offered to make a relief panel from the silhouette as my contribution to the 1981 "Work Week" at the school, thus adding an additional hurdle—the necessity of working against a deadline. The only drawing approximating the desired size had been used for a banner, which was far away in Raleigh. There was a metal cutout on the school sign, so this was copied on a 1-in (2.54-cm) sheet of plastic foam, cleaned up, and reversed by photocopying portions and assembling them. Then began the laborious job of drawing in detail, which started with the discovery that the rear horse had only three legs and that there was no plough. This was confirmed next day when a 50-year-old Danish woodcarving of a man ploughing was produced, and when Murray Martin, a retired woodcarving instructor at Brasstown, came up with a $2\frac{1}{2}$-in (6.4-cm) brooch depicting the same scene—one of three cast in Denmark perhaps 50 years ago. It also bore more of the legend: "I am a common farmer, I sing behind the plough, I am happy and free." The brooch was too small to show all necessary detail, but permitted roughing-in of the figure details and started me guessing as to the rest. Some research in old books helped on harness detail, which was further improved by the recollections of two visitors who had ploughed with two-horse teams in their youth in nearby Georgia and Mississippi. Meanwhile, I had begun trenching for the silhouette, which took a day or two. I arbitrarily decided on a depth of ½ in (13 mm) and maintained uniformity with a brad driven into a stick to make a gauge.

The area around Brasstown is mountainous, and the top of the 3-piece panel assembled by the Cabinet Shop contained a white top of growth wood; so I bandsawed away the "sky" to leave some light-topped hills, as if a lowering sun were hitting them. Lettering 2 in (5.1 cm) tall was laid out to form a base cup for the carving, and to center the important third of the quotation on the bottom—this necessitated adding the word "for" to the third line. That seemed a minor change, because a translation of the original Danish by J. C. Auberg is quite different from the previously quoted lines.

Modelling the figures took four days and four long evenings. I decided to cut away the background to trenching depth at the top, leaving the full depth at the base and half-sides in which to incise the lettering with a V-tool. Background above the lettering was textured with a flat gouge and some texturing was done on the bodies of the horses to avoid shine from flat surfaces. The finished carving was given one coat of Deft® to seal it, then an old can of fruitwood color stain was discovered and used for antiquing. This took another day and a half, leaving a half-day to drill and file hangers, find wire and test the carving in its location over a fireplace.

Fig. 100. Commemorative relief panel in walnut, based—in part—on an old silhouette.

CHAPTER XIV

The Kubbestol—A One-Piece Tradition

Scandinavian block stool is a carver's challenge

THE KUBBESTOL IS A VERY OLD FORM OF BLOCK—or solid—stool, made in Scandinavia from a hollowed tree trunk. Early ones were low-backed, with little or no decoration, but those made in Minnesota resemble a chair, with both the back and solid skirt decorated with relief carving.

This stool was made from a section of the trunk of an ash—carved green. A 3-ft (0.9-m) length, 16 in (41 cm) in diameter, was cut halfway through in the middle, and one half was then split away. I used a chain saw to cut a series of radial segments in the remaining half, and split them out to leave a 2-in (5-cm) ring of living wood for the back. Then the chain saw, with a 14-in (36-cm) arm, was used to plunge-cut a central plug out of the solid base, about 1½ saw-widths on a side. This is much harder than it sounds, because the saw tends to run instead of cutting, and it overloads as well. We drove out the heart plug with a sledge, and I immediately stripped the bark and rounded up the hole with a 2½-in (6.4-cm) flat spade gouge, since ash will check overnight and removal of the heart wood inhibits that action (at least to a degree).

The original log weighed about 175 lb (79 kg). With the core removed, it was reduced to about 80 lb (36 kg). Next day, minor checks showed around both ends of the solid skirt section, but these did not progress; in fact, they eventually closed as more of the interior wood was removed. I did not 'attempt to round up the skirt because I wanted to maintain diameter and strength as well as provide some interest in the shape. Wood was removed with a 1-in (2.54-cm) carpenter's gouge and a 2½-in (6.4-cm) flat gouge in a continuous process around the interior. When the walls and back were approximately 1½ in (3.8 cm) thick, the bottom end was cut true and smoothed. The top was rough-shaped to design, then thinning was continued. At this point, the stool was 33½ in (85 cm) high and roughly 14 in (36 cm) in diameter, with a seat height of 15½ in (39 cm). When wall thickness was down to 1 in (2.54 cm), it weighed 30 lb (14 kg) and had no visible checks.

Figs. 101–102. The Scandinavian Kubbestol, or block stool, has been made for centuries. This one is more elaborate than usual, with most surfaces carved. It is ash, about 14 × 33 in (36 × 84 cm), and weighs 24 lb (11 kg). Seat is red Naugahyde® atop plywood. Back view (right) points up benefits of antiquing with dark stain, painted on interstices and lines and then rubbed away. This provides surface contrast and emphasizes the patterns, along with the shape of the log itself and darker streaks in the grain.

From various references, I gathered designs for Odin (or Wotan), Thor and Freyr (sons of Odin), Freya (sister of Freyr) and Frigga (Odin's wife). To finish, I needed a Valkyrie, a female warrior who brought the bravest of the fallen heroes to Valhalla. The gods were spaced around the skirt, with Thor positioned front and center. This was because my design had the god placed on a natural bulge of the wood, and his two goats, Tanngnjost and Tanngrisir, in a hollow where I'd left a little inner bark—which would give them a variation in tone and texture.

Odin was the most powerful of the Norse gods. He invented poetry, liked history and sacrificed one eye for wisdom. His pet ravens, Hugin and Munin (or Thought and Memory), flew daily to the four corners of the universe to bring him its secrets. He was also the god of the dead to whom the Valkyries brought the souls of slain heroes to live again in his banquet hall. Odin also invented writing and the runes, peculiar letter forms that are thought to be derived from the practice of divining by throwing sticks—they are patterns of short straight lines such as thrown sticks might make.

I incised the name of each god and added a line of runes in the band at the front of the seat. The line is simply a phonetic translation of a toast I made up: "May you sit in the laps of the gods." For the outside designs, I arbitrarily decided to sink the background ¼ in (6.4 mm), so it was a natural for a power router—which took only three hours for the entire job. However, setting-in the recessed areas of the irregular face and cleaning up the background around each figure took a couple of days. I found that a deep gouge (fluter), with about a ³⁄₁₆-in (5-mm) curve at the bottom and high parallel sides, could be driven along the lines to avoid the usual veiner outlining and wearisome setting-in. It leaves a small radius at the base which is desirable in many instances and is not visible after antiquing, anyway. For this, I use a very light mallet so that the tools never overcut or overstress the wood surface. Also, I use smaller and smaller firmers and gouges as the work progresses—even down to ⅛- and ¼-in (3.2- and 6.4-mm) widths.

Ash will support considerable detail if tools are kept sharp and you take it easy. The wood has a tendency to leave small, fuzzy splinters on occasion, and these must be removed almost individually. (I know a sign carver who uses a blowtorch for this purpose, thus saving a considerable amount of time.) Also, on my blank there was a strip of dead wood and one area that had been attacked by insects. This area required more careful cutting than the rest and the holes had to be filled with glue and sawdust. I usually pour the glue into the hole, then pile sawdust on top and knead it down. That's much easier than working with a gluey mixture. After a few minutes, the surplus sawdust can be blown off.

My sketches included a considerable amount of detail, probably more than you will want to put in. I eliminated a few fine points here and there as I carved because they were not essential and were beyond the capacity of the wood grain or surface to take.

For the surface carving, I used ⅟₁₆-, ⅛-and ¼-in (1.6-, 3.2- and 6.4-mm) firmers, and similar small gouges of various radii, alternating with a sharp-pointed knife. Details of faces and hands, the lining of beards, and the heads of the animals were knife jobs for me, as was the rounding of axle spokes, horns and such, but I used the veiner and V-tool as much as possible because they are much faster. Even so, each god-design took the better part of a day. Just for kicks, I used an ornamental brass upholstery tack for the central boss of the Viking's shield, and put black gimp tacks as center bosses in two Viking shields on the ship. The ship, by the way, was positioned so that the handhole came in the center of the sail. For all this work, it is easier and faster to transfer the tool from hand to hand than to move the piece. It takes some practice, but it can be done. Doing the designs on the inside of the back was something else again, because of the extreme curvature. Most of the design could be outlined with a ⅛-in (3.2-mm) round gouge and close details outlined with a veiner, but I found that a short-bent gouge was essential in some areas. The short-bent gouge was too long to use with the mallet for short distances, particularly near the top where the back "ears" come so far forward. The tool could be used alone, however, by pushing and rotating it—somewhat akin to what an engraver does with a burin. Setting-in the background was comparatively easy because cuts could be made with a flat gouge along the grain for most of it, and the rest removed with small flat gouges (although near the seat area it may be necessary to have the arm holding the chisel come up through the skirt).

The conventional Kubbestol, by the way, has a flat wooden seat cut to the inner contour of the skirt top and tapered slightly so that it can be wedged and nailed in place. I elected, instead, to have a thin plywood seat, recessed about ½ in (13 mm) so that a foam-padded cushion could be set in. The plywood could have been held by cleats, but I wanted to thin the top of the skirt anyway, so I decided to cut a ½-in (13-mm) step ¾ in (19 mm) deep all around. I made this step only approximately level, because I wanted air spaces around the edge of the plywood to avoid a differential-humidity problem inside the skirt when the chair was set on a rug—which would effectively seal the bottom. An alternate design would have been simply to drill a few small holes in the plywood seat, but that would have been hard on the cushion.

The cushion, by the way, was made of three ½-in (13-mm) layers of discarded foam plastic from an ironing board, covered with a dark-red vinyl. My wife decided that it should be a welted rather than a boxed edge, so the welting would just cover the inside edge of the skirt. The cushion was made to a cardboard pattern, painstakingly cut to fit.

Light sanding with a worn-out piece of fine sandpaper removed most of the burrs and slivers on the piece; a pocketknife took care of the difficult ones. The ground was not smoothed but was left with flat-gouge lines showing, while the surfaces of the designs and the borders were smoothed. Further, as each design was completed, it was sprayed with satin varnish to protect it against grime. All surfaces were finally sprayed with a second coat. Then a teak oil stain was applied and immediately rubbed off flat surfaces, to leave the darker color in carved lines and adjacent to the pieces, thus creating an antiqued effect. This required some touch-up here and there with a small brush, as well as some scraping where too much stain was absorbed, but the spray varnish makes such touch-ups relatively easy.

The inside of the skirt was also varnished to equalize surfaces, as was the underside of the seat, which, by the way, was oak-faced plywood (which approximates the ash in color and figure when varnished). Before inside varnishing, some additional slivers were removed from behind the figures to cut weight and equalize wood thickness to some degree, so final weight is about 23 lb (10 kg) without the cushion, and wood thickness is about ¾ in (19 mm). As a final finish, an additional spray coat of satin varnish covered the stain, followed in turn by two coats of wax and a final top coat of neutral Kiwi® shoe polish buffed with a soft-bristle shoebrush, which gives a slightly higher gloss than the wax. The result is a chair with a warm tan-to-brown color range and a surface which exudes soft reflections and shows the carving quite clearly.

Fig. 103. This 80-lb (36-kg) rough shows chain-saw marks, has 2-in (5-cm) walls and required one day to produce. Core hole was plunge-cut with a chain saw, then interior and exterior surfaces were shaped with 1- and 2½-in (2.54- and 6.4-cm) gouges.

Fig. 104. Progressive shaping and thinning brought walls down to 1½ in (3.8 cm). Some inner bark was left in hollows of the naturally contoured skirt, in the event that the darker tone would help design.

Fig. 105. Six designs were spaced around the skirt, scroll-banded at the top and plain-banded at bottom. Similar scroll-banding at back enclosed two Vikings that flank a scene symbolizing the origin of man, with a Viking ship across the waist. Here the background has been routed ¼ in (6.4 mm) deep.

Fig. 106. After mechanical routing, design outlines were detailed and areas bosted where the router could not reach. Also, a ¼-in (6.4-mm) ledge was cut inside top of skirt down ¾ in (19 mm), to support a ¼-in (6.4-mm) contoured plywood seat and leave a ½-in (13-mm) rim to enclose the padded cushion. Weight is now 30 lb (14 kg).

Figs. 107–108 (below and right). Back was carved first. It was necessary to plug and tone an area just over the head of Aske, the first man (Embla was the first woman).

Extend limbs to fill area

HUMAN CREATION
Man made from an ash tree, woman from an alder.

Note that figures are not completed

Fig. 109 (right). Drape lines of Frigga's skirt are established with small gouge cuts and then faired in. Wool on distaff is suggested by veiner lines. Frigga was Odin's wife and queen of Asgard, patroness of ships, and brought lovers together after death. With her is Fulla, keeper of her jewels.

Fig. 110 (above). Freya was the most propitious of the goddesses, who loved music, flowers, fairies and elves, so human lovers invoked her. She is usually shown driving a chariot drawn by cats and is sometimes confused with Frigga or even Saga, goddess of poetry. Freya was Odin's daughter and Freyr's sister.

Figs. 111–112 (left and above). Thor, the Thunderer, and Freyr, Odin's sons. Thor's chariot is drawn by Tanngnjost and Tann-grisir, his goats; note that bark is left on them for texture and tint. Freyr, or Frey (above), god of the sun, is usually shown riding high over the mountains on a boar—thus, his image is placed high on the skirt, with mountain range in miniature along base line.

Fig. 113 (right). Symbol on inside back of Kubbestol is the Norse sign for eternal life, said to have been the favorite design of Helen Keller because she could trace it with her fingertips. Gods on the stool are identified by runic characters, a very old alphabet said to be derived from the thrown sticks used in divining. Germany and Scandinavia used it as early as the fourth century.

Fig. 114. Odin (Wotan, Woden) was the principal Norse god, but not the first, nor, indeed, the Supreme Being. He ruled the universe and gathered fallen heroes for an ultimate battle with the giants. His wolves are Geri and Freki, and his ravens, Hugin and Munin (Thought and Memory). This is the largest and most detailed motif and is placed at the center rear of the skirt, where a broad arcuate surface was available.

VALKYRIE ("Chooser of the Slain")
(ᚦᚨᛚᚲᚨᚱᛁᛊ)

Note: Norse warriors wore chain-mail shirts

Fig. 115.

Figs. 115–116. The Valkyries (Choosers of the Slain) were messengers for Odin and brought the bravest of fallen heroes to Valhalla, Odin's banquet hall in Asgard, after their veil of death was removed in the forest of Glasir. A Valkyrie wore a chain mail shirt and a winged helmet that enabled her and her horse to fly. She was armed with a spear, and her armor shed a strange flickering light—the Aurora Borealis.

Figs. 117–118 (above and below). The Viking ship was low in the waist and high at prow and stern, both often decorated. Though shallow-keeled, it was fairly seaworthy and was apparently the last survivor of Roman and Greek designs in northern Europe. Crews ranged from 30 to 60, a third at the oars—which were used much more than the awkward square sail—the other two-thirds ready to fight, with their shields draped along the bulwarks. It was steered by an oar at stern right.

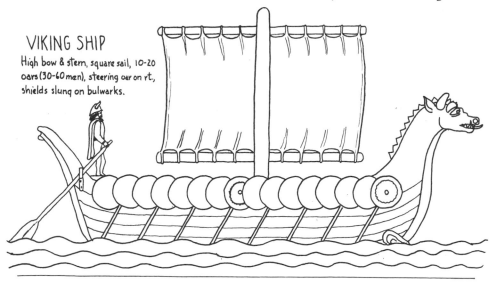

VIKING SHIP
High bow & stern, square sail, 10-20 oars (30-60 men), steering oar on rt., shields slung on bulwarks.

CHAPTER XV

Ecology II—A 6-Panel Door

478 flora and fauna carved in teak polyglot panels

EVER SINCE I BEGAN TO CARVE THE "BUG TREE" back in the mid-sixties, I have been fascinated by polyglot grouping of low-relief subjects without any elaborate background or tracery to connect them. There are infinite possibilities, and I have only begun to explore them in more than a score of panels. Not all of these polyglot carvings were on flat panels; I have carved on a half-dozen wooden shoes, a walrus tusk or two and many other surfaces. The subjects have included flora and fauna, vegetables and fruits, musical instruments, toys, fabulous figures—anything in which there are a number of readily recognizable shape variations. I have even mixed flowers and birds successfully. One carver wrote me that she carves only shoes of all vintages, and so she carved various shoes on a wooden shoe.

This series of six panels is my best example. They are in teak, and vary in size as well as thickness. The eight panels I carved for a door eleven years ago were in an essentially rotary design, around a central doorknob—which most of us don't have. This is a vertical grouping on a more conventional door. I had a piece of 4/4 teak, a piece 1¼ in (3.2 cm) thick and another 1⅜ in (3.5 cm), which could be combined into a 1¼ in (3.2-cm) whole, so these pieces were the basic elements. It took some scrambling to find more teak, but I got a ¾ × 9⅜-in (1.9 × 24-cm) plank 13½ ft (4.1 m) long— at a bit over $100! About half of it made the four smaller panels. The group had to be relatively narrow, because the front door on which the panels were to be placed was to be covered year-round by a glass storm door, and the knob was of course on one side. The grouping is flexible, so panels could be

Fig. 119. Six teak panels are combined on a plain pine door to display 478 species of local fauna and flora in mid-New York State. Panels vary in thickness as well as size.

set any distance apart, from zero to perhaps 3 in (7.6 cm). I figured on 4½-in (11-cm) clearance on sides and top, 6 in (15 cm) at bottom to clear an inadvertent kick. Because the house is in the country, I chose flowers, trees (leaves), birds, bugs, local animals and fresh-water fish as my subjects.

Sizes of elements and subjects can suit your own purposes and design; they are, however, dependent to some degree upon your ability to draw. It is easier to trace them directly from references such as field handbooks, though these tend to standardize the size and pose because of the standard illustration size. Better and more versatile are the lengthier texts, including books for children, which will show larger and more varied poses than the usual handbook top views of insects and side views of animals and fish. I trace from the original when the size is suitable, using a scratch awl (to avoid marking up the book) and carbon paper directly on the wood, then strengthening the outline with a soft-point pen.

I find it best *not* to design the entire panel in advance. I trace or copy the designs as they seem to fit, and stay roughly one row ahead of my carving. That keeps me from forgetting details of the designs and then inadvertently cutting off a leg. Further, it reduces the likelihood of missing lines in copying, and the possibility that the design will be partially erased by the friction of my hands and arms over it. I also find on teak that the oil in the wood has a tendency to fade drawn lines over a period of time.

In the sizes with which I work, I am not concerned about relative scale of various elements. An eagle may be 5 in (13 cm) long, a wren or humming-bird 2 in (5.1 cm), and they may be side by side. Any attempt to maintain scale would result in highly disproportionate units. Besides, when you're copying directly from texts, scale is not constant either.

In these sizes, the tools must be small. I have perhaps ten chisels ready, but some are almost never used. The ½-in (13-mm) firmer, for example, is useless except for smoothing a surface. Tools used constantly are the V-tool, 1/16-in (1.6-mm) and ⅛-in (3.2-mm) flat gouges and a hook knife. Less frequent is the need for the veiner, ¼-in (6.4-mm) firmer, ¼-in (6.4-mm) gouges of several sweeps, a ⅛-in (3.2-mm) fluter and a regular pocketknife. Many of the areas are so small that miniature tools would be a help. Always remember the sizes of your smallest tools and the character of the wood when you design; if you don't, you'll have excessive splitting and breakage.

Polyglot panels are a particularly good exercise in using the V-tool because there are endless leaf veins, fish fins, bird and insect wings to be lined—a job usually too fine for the average veiner. You may also want to do some texturing, such as cross-hatching, and there is inevitably the need for separating planes. By tilting the V-tool to one side, you can cut a vertical wall on one side and a longer slope on the other, making the side with the long slope appear below the one with the vertical wall. The tool is also handy for cleaning out around a design after grounding-out, notching vertical walls to suggest a ragged edge and a variety of other purposes. But you must keep it sharp.

When notching or grooving fine lines, I hold the V-tool by the blade as I would a pencil, making the cut with the fingers alone. The length and direction of the stroke are thus controlled more precisely. Precision and control can be further enhanced by gripping the panel with the other hand so the middle fingers of the tool hand press against the thumb or index finger of the holding hand to act as a stop. (I intentionally avoided using the designations "left" and "right" because you should learn to make such cuts with either hand, thus saving board rotation.) To carve panels like these, I either lay them flat on a bench or prop them against the bench with the lower end on my knees, sitting down whenever possible. This makes panel position much more flexible, and the panel is usually big enough to stay in place without clamping. When at an angle, the panel will also rid itself of most of the chips as you work.

The hook or pull knife is also particularly useful on work like this because the heel of the blade will not nick adjacent surfaces, the point is narrow and the concavity makes it stay in the cut rather than jump out on occasion (although it does tend to jump free at an edge).

It is possible to shortcut the usual lengthy procedure of outlining and grounding-out, because most elements are round-edged somewhat anyway. I do not outline with the V-tool before setting-in. My designs tend to be small, so a 1/8-in (3.2-mm) firmer will handle most of the setting-in except for sharp curves. I set-in less than 1/8 in (3.2 mm) on the first pass, depending on the wood. (Teak tends to crush and splinter if the tool is driven in deep enough to cause serious sidewise wedging.) I remove the waste, then set-in again. Also, all setting-in is done with a light mallet. I find I develop a pattern of blows (two or three taps with the grain, three or four across it), which makes the work go fast.

In panels like these, it is unnecessary to get the entire background bosted to the same depth or even maintain a precise plane surface. This is because the background areas are quite small and are eventually stained dark anyway, so a little unevenness will help avoid the light reflection given by a flat surface. It is also unnecessary to texture these backgrounds, thus saving time.

On large panels, I bost the background down a bit over ⅛ in (3.2 mm). This is deep enough with background staining and makes undercutting unnecessary. If the area is small or complex, I set-in in three steps to reduce crushing of delicate elements. Obviously, you can't set-in the two sides of a thin element such as an insect leg or antenna in the conventional way. If the section is very narrow, particularly across-grain, I set-in with a knife and may ground-out with it as well. On teak, any section less than about ¼ in (6.4 mm)—particularly across-grain—must be treated with great care. Setting-in can be done with the chisel on almost all sections if you slope the tool edge away from the vertical on the second side and set-in in three or four passes. This leaves a sloping side that can then be cut vertical safely because the obstructing wood outside is gone.

My custom is to set-in larger areas first as far as possible and skip over the interior bosting between two adjacent slender sections. Then I go back, pray, and do the small areas. You may find it advisable to leave extremely slender sections a bit over-width initially, slimming them down with the hook knife as you complete carving. It may also be possible to put a mark on the major setting-in tool tips to indicate the desired setting-in depth, but then you'll have to renew the line every time you sharpen the tool.

Try to keep in mind the cutting problems as you lay out the panel. Leave yourself enough space to clear your smallest tools. Adjoining subjects should be as different in shape and size as possible. A panel of fish, for example, tends to be monotonous because so many of the subjects will be generally similar in shape and positioned horizontally; break it up with angled poses, leaping fish or even a crab or turtle. Also, a panel containing birds, which have a recognizably similar conformation, must also attain interest by the use of variety in pose. Further, all birds have bills that usually end in a point, so if the bill is across-grain, it is edgy to carve. (Of course, if you get the bills with the grain, the legs will be across it—so you can't win!)

You can avoid some of the grief with legs by having flying or sitting birds, or by arranging poses so that the legs of one bird are apparently behind the body or wing of another. With insects, observing grain for six legs and two antennae is impossible particularly because they stick out at odd angles and tend to curve. Some support can be gained by intersecting them, overlapping them or having long antennae or legs run across an adjacent body or wing— thus vastly reducing the cutting depth necessary. In most cases, antennae and legs, especially on insects, are so small that only undetailed general shape is necessary, without such projection as fuzz, kinky joints and such. Besides, such details will not be seen on a large panel.

You may have a problem grouping elements and deciding which details to include. Should this leg extend over that animal's back? What do you do about the long antennae of some insects, the long tail of a bird of paradise? The coward's way out is not to include difficult subjects. Mine is to draw the subjects where I think they belong, showing overlaps. Then I decide each situation as I reach it, often placing a leg over an adjacent wing to reduce the depth of cut.

When laying out a polyglot panel, it is very important to make a record of each subject as it is drawn in. I simply draw approximate blob shapes on a pad in approximate position, and write across the blob the name of the subject, the reference (A, B, C, etc.) and the page number. Then when I do detail carving, I can find it again quickly. This also serves as the base for the ultimate identification key and helps avoid including different poses of the same subject drawn from different references. The key, by the way, can be tied in with an approximate tracing of the finished panel, with numbers written on an enlargement of the photograph of it or on a tracing made over the photo.

Border width can be what you wish; I find that about ⅝ in (16 mm) looks good and allows room to drill for the fastening screws. These, by the way, are No. 8 1½-in (3.8-cm) brass flathead screws, set in recessed holes and capped by plugs of the same wood glued in to match the grain, then sanded smooth and finished. Screw holes are oversize to allow slight shifting if either door or panel is affected by humidity.

Panels can be almost any shape or size, and can be made up of individual subjects alone. What you use depends upon purpose and time. Out of curiosity, I kept records on this door panel by panel. Total carving time was about 375 hours, of which 25 were general preparation of boards, obtaining materials, planning of the door design and drilling screw holes and installation. The flower panel, for example, required 113½ hours and contains 162 designs, while the animal panel (smallest of the group) took 33½ hours and included 41 subjects. All were done roughly in order of increasing difficulty. Layout time, in two cases, was 17 percent of the total for the panel while carving time was a bit under an hour per subject, ranging from 1.06 to 1.6 units per hour. (I carve relatively quickly, so your time may not be as good— as it is with m.p.g. estimates for present-day cars.) It is also interesting to note that these six panels include 478 separate designs, as compared with

459 in the eight panels of the larger door I did eleven years earlier. This indicates that I had a more compact layout in this case, probably because I used more designs directly from references without enlargement.

As you may know, in the elaborate panelling and pierced-work carving in medieval churches, the monks and their lay assistants occasionally worked in designs that are secular and sometimes even bawdy. This was also true of the single designs for misericords—the little projections under fold-up church seats upon which weary buttocks could be rested during lengthy periods when church attendees were ostensibly standing—several of which are illustrated in my book, *Carving Religious Motifs in Wood*. This was probably to relieve the tedium of carving endless vines and religious symbols. Something similar occurred in these panels. Thus, you will find a tree frog basking on a basswood leaf in the tree panel, a sea horse, a crustacean and a sea snake (saurian) among the fish, as well as The Little Mermaid—definitely a mammal. Among the animals are domestic beasts, and among the insects are two spiders and a mite, all arachnids, a worm or two, a fish (being juice-sucked by an insect) and even the White Rock girl; she is watching a frog catch a dismayed damselfly. Among the flowers are a snail, an inchworm, a snake and a female gnome collecting Dutchman's-breeches. Not exactly formal, but why not? They give an added fillip to the careful searcher. A doodlebug catching an ant, a tarantula hawk stinging a tarantula, an insect attacking a fish, the White Rock girl watching the frog—these are all little scenes incorporated in the panel. They relieve the monotony and expand your experience.

Fig. 120. Flower panel is 1-in (2.54-cm) teak, tree panel comprises two glued pieces 1¼ in (3.2 cm) thick, and fish panel is ¾ × 9⅜ in (1.9 × 24 cm) wide. Flower panel is the largest of all six.

*Fig. 121. All three of these panels are ¾-in (19-mm) teak 9⅜ in (24 cm) wide.
Insect panel is most complex of the group because of antennae and legs.*

Figs. 122–123 (left and below). Layout of elements is done just ahead of grounding and modelling, as these examples show. Immediate completion assists recollection of design and provides step-by-step satisfaction.

Fig. 124. This panel was a design test for my first ecology door in 1970.

CHAPTER XVI

How to Carve Lettering

Design is as complex as execution

LETTERING ON A CARVING may have one or more purposes. It can be just a signature and/or date, a title, a dedication, or the major subject of the carving itself. If you carve a likeness, you will almost certainly want to add a title. The Arabic alphabet is cursive (script) and flowing, thus lends itself to endless variations and is easy to incorporate in a design, but our Roman alphabet is rigid and much more difficult to use. Once it consisted only of capitals, and before that simply incised strokes, but the addition of lower-case letters for ease of reading, and of the running-hand, cursive or script forms for easier handwriting, tremendously complicated the job of the carver. Today we have vertical letters and sloping letters (italics), and many alphabets have weighted lines and curves and lines to end each basic stroke. These letter terminals are called *serifs* and are a major problem in relief carving, particularly across grain. Also, letterers add flourishes called *swashes* to the tails of letters—as some penmen do—or make elaborate tails and loops called *uncials*.

All this does not mean that any lettering you do must be elaborate—or boring. You can vary the designs to suit your purpose, as long as the letters are recognizable and legible, and you can finish them in many ways. The effect of raised lettering can be achieved by stamping or otherwise texturing the background around it; letters can be outlined (if they are large enough), inlaid or even carved with channels or grooves in the wider verticals of capital letters. But the easiest form is V-groove incising, particularly if the wood and the tool sharpness permit use of the veiner or V-tool, or you are working in end grain. You *can* go all out and do raised lettering as a continuous cursive strip, as if a ribbon had been laid on the surface to form the letters. If you undertake that, be prepared for trouble, and except no sympathy from me. It is my firm belief that much lettering on carvings, particularly titles, is unnecessary and looks crude, even if the carving itself is well done. If you must have elegant lettering, have it engraved or etched on a brass or silver appliqued plate.

Even the simplest lettering is difficult to carve. The difficulties include line width, spacing and depth, and increase with smaller size and more complex letter forms, such as serifs and swashes, as well as if the letters must project rather than be incised, because the eye picks up very small variations in the curve, spacing or width of a line. Further, calligraphy—the design and execution of ornamental lettering—is rising in public favor, so many people are more conscious of letter forms.

It is a paradox that the typewriter and most other forms of commercial type place each letter in a block of uniform width and height, while the calligrapher and the handsetter consider a great many spacing variations essential. Small wonder that carvers go to templates and routers to produce passable lettering!

There are an endless number of rules that the sign painter and the hand typesetter, as well as the calligrapher, follow. Some of the simpler ones are: The letters i and l require only ½ space, while the letters m and w require 1½; a punctuation mark requires ½, with a single space between words and at least a double space between sentences. Letters that are very boxy, like capital H, need ½ space between, but rounded ones like O, P and Q can be crowded closer to adjacent letters. Letters like o and c actually look smaller in a line of type than do many others, so they can be made slightly taller. A letter like t, particularly a capital T, can be crowded slightly closer to adjacent letters like o or a because of the projecting crossbar on top. This is also true of the letter f on its right side. Interline spacing can vary widely, from one-half the total line width to more than twice the line width, but line spacing should be widened as line length or letter weight increases, for ease of reading.

There are many other rules, some of which will vary with the particular alphabet being used. For example, in the large plaque pictured (Fig. 125), the t, l, and f are special forms requiring a full space in width. My best suggestion for the beginner at carving letters is to use a simple sans serif alphabet. Gothic, script, italic and archaic alphabets are much harder to carve well.

There are occasions when all these suggestions must be abandoned, as in designing and carving the legend of the bird (Fig. 135). This is the old Celtic story, so it seemed appropriate to design it with an alphabet from *The Book of Kells*, and to use a decorative band from that book as well.

My first idea was a simple carving of the bird suspended from a thorn, the whole composition "white on white" except for a vermilion drop of blood.

Fig. 125 (above). Gothic letters in relief, Spanish, 14th or 15th century. Fig. 126 (below). Gothic letters from the tomb of Richard II, and others, about 1400.

Fig. 127 (above). Incised letters from the Forum at Rome. Fig. 128 (below). Elizabethan lettering from an incised inscription at North Walsham, Norfolk, England.

ABCDEFGHIKLMNP
QRSTWY! 1234567890
abcdefghjkmprstuvwxyz

Fig. 129 (above). Engraver's Old English.

ABCDEFGHIJKLM
NOPQRSTUVWXYZ

Fig. 130. Modern initials.

ABCDEFGHIJKLMNOPQRSTU
VWXYZ&   1234567890$
abcdefghijklmnopqrstuvwxyz

Fig. 131. Caslon Old-Style alphabet, the basis for numerous modern type faces.

ABCDEFGHIJKLMNOP
QRSTUVWXYZ&
abcdefghijklmnopqrstuv
wxyz   1234567890$

Fig. 132. Ultra-Bodoni Italic; note slant and extra-fat letters.

ABCDEFGHIJKLMNOPQRSTUV
WXYZ&   1234567890$
abcdefghijklmnopqrstuvwxyz

Fig. 133. Sans Serif, which must be carefully spaced between letters for ease in reading.

Then I realized that the carving might well be meaningless to most people, and the legend itself should be included. This suggested that the plaque take the form of an illuminated manuscript, with the bird as the ornamental initial. It seemed advisable to include some other decoration for the "page" as well, so the idea of including a side band combined with the thorn branch was born. Fortunately, the ancient Celts were fond of designs of vines growing from pots, so the branch could simply be an extension. It could also incorporate some of the complex patterns the Celts used in the bird itself, so I braided the extended tail.

My original plan was to carry the thorn branch out to form an ornamental T and to begin the legend with the words, "There was once a bird . . ." This would have necessitated a tag line at the end "—Celtic legend," which can be hard to handle, and the words did not fit well in the line width. So I converted the opening to the present one and avoided both problems. The word "Celtic" gives a better start than the rather flat "There," and the thorn branch could make a C as readily as a T. Also, the word "bards" is a bit more graphic than the word "legends," which would have crowded the line anyway.

The second line presented a similar problem: If the bird were considered impersonal, I might have used "that" instead of "who." And so it went through the quotation. My point is that unless a quotation must be exact, it is possible to rewrite it slightly as you go to avoid splitting a word or over-spacing words; hyphens and gaps don't look well in a line. I was, of course, trying to make all the lines the same overall length. Typographers and cryptographers avoid this problem by having one edge or the other of the column "ragged"—that is, they allow the lines to come as nearly as possible to the desired width, but to vary slightly on one side, usually the right. (This would have been perfectly possible in this case, because the alignment needed only to be with the band at the left.

Another alternative, for short quotations or lettering, is to center each line, thus leaving both edges ragged. A third alternative is to increase the width of each letter, or the spaces between letters and words, to make the line come out even (note the difference, for example, in the spaces between words on the bird panel from line to line). A fourth alternative is to reduce letter size slightly after the first few lines; this is common in newspapers and similar printing, but less common among typographers (note that my fifth and subsequent lines are slightly smaller).

In addition, there is the problem of the space between design and lettering. On the sixth line I elected to split the difference between the lengths of preceding and following lines; it could have been the width of the line above (leaving an unsightly space below the bird), or as long as the succeeding line (crowding the design too much). These are, of course, very much matters of personal opinion and taste.

There is also the matter of lettering size and spacing. In this case, I used a ⅜-in (9.5-mm) letter height for capitals, which gave the lower-case letters a basic height of ¼ in (6.3 mm), plus "upstanders" and "downstanders," as they are called. The spacing between lines is also ¼ in (6.3 mm), which is enough as long as an upstander on one letter doesn't exactly meet the downstander of another. I was lucky.

The old Celtic alphabet had no k, and its capital G looked something like a reversed capital F. You will note that the little wedge-line atop the t and g is higher than the line of letters, and that the f is slightly higher and adds a downstander (which our alphabets, except the script, have lost). Also, the s has a larger loop on top than on the bottom. All of these things further complicate the lettering design and execution. I replaced the capital G with a more modern form, added the k and changed the ampersand to a later design in the interest of readability, but I left the i as it originally was, without the dot above, because the dot is a nuisance anyway.

I have gone into considerable detail here on design, because books on lettering design are not readily available, at least in my experience. There are, however, books showing alphabets, as well as lettering catalogs and the like, from which you can select. I repeat my original injunction: Pick a simple alphabet, at least initially. Gothic and flowery lettering is not designed for the carver but for the penman and illustrator, and most woods won't take the detail, even if your eyes and tools will. And incise your lettering, unless you have endless time and patience. Incised letters can be tinted easily for legibility, by simply putting on a stop coat of varnish and flowing a paint or stain into the lettering then wiping off the excess as a scrimshander does on ivory. (If the surface of the piece is tinted by the coloring, it can be lightly sanded to clean it up, but you can't do that with raised lettering!)

Because thin plastic sheet can be molded to almost any form and will pick up even surface roughness and grain lines, some carvers have had commissions to produce patterns for such work. These patterns are often in woods that will display a decided grain, like oak, particularly with a little sandblasting after carving. Sign carvers also make use of this characteristic of wood, sandblasting their lettering after completion to give it a weathered look. It is also quite common to batter the sign a bit with a chain or other flexible but hard object to add to the weathering, as well as to do some scorching with a blowtorch (which incidentally removes burrs and feather edges, and makes sanding unnecessary).

The "MDA 7" shown here (Fig. 136) is in this category. It was produced in white pine with raised and serifed lettering to serve as a pattern in clay or Plasticine. Because it was to be applied directly to the material, which had to read correctly, the pattern had to be in reverse and also had to have slightly sloping sides so it could be withdrawn after it was pressed into the material.

Another problem that you may face on occasion is to produce a monogram. This is usually composed of three letters, but may be two or four, or even more in the case of a company or an individual who carries a "Junior" or "III," for example. The simplest approach is to make the letter of the Christian name dominant, with the other two laced over it. Because so many letters in the English alphabet have vertical and horizontal lines, this is relatively easy. A dominant circular letter like c or o can enclose the others, or one with a space at top and/or bottom, like m, n, or w, can do the same.

Sometimes one letter can serve to complete another, as in the initials AGA, in which the G can tie together the two A's, one over the other, by forming the crossbars as it cuts through both. Of course, modern printers avoid the entire problem by putting the letters in order, vertically, horizontally or diagonally, but the calligrapher interlocks them in one way or another, even if he or she must modify the letter form to do it.

Fig. 134. Dog 1¼ × 9 × 10 in (3.2 × 23 × 25 cm) is set on a base 4½ × 13 in (11 × 33 cm), with forward bevel that reads: "Lord, help me this day to keep my nose out of other people's business."

Fig. 135 (right). Panel in English sycamore (harewood), about 12 × 16 in (30 × 41 cm), has incised lettering combined with a trenched low-relief of a bird impaled on a thorn, which also provides an initial letter C. Thorn grows from a Celtic interlaced potted-tree design forming the left border. The alphabet is Celtic, with some additions to make it understandable today.

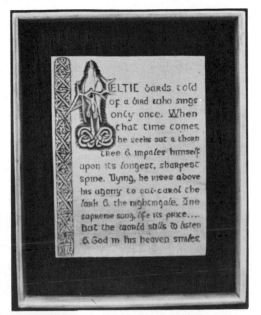

Fig. 136 (left). Serifed and weighted letters provide a pattern for clay impressions. Letters must have sloping sides to pull from the clay. Wood is white pine, and overall size is 2 × 7½ in (5.1 × 19 cm).

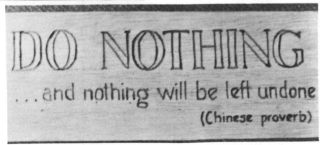

Fig. 137. Simple incised and serifed lettering, with weighted verticals, forms the first line of this desk block. Second and third lines are simple incising. All lines are filled with pigment, after which the surface is sanded (as in scrimshaw) and then matte-varnished.

111

CHAPTER XVII
Lettering an Award Panel

Carved elements appliqued, caption data incised

AWARDS OF ONE KIND OR ANOTHER lend themselves particularly to wood-carving, and can range from a simple shaped plaque for a background to something that includes likenesses. Almost always, however, unless the award incorporates an engraved plate, some lettering will be required, and some research will be necessary.

This example (Fig. 141) is one of the more elaborate panels I've done, presented to a man on his 55th birthday. The client suggested the general form: an indication of the subject's college background, indicated by initial letters and mascots, and his professional life to date.

The first step in designing such a panel is to do the research. In this case, I had to find out the shape of the Princeton letter P, the Columbia letter C, and the New York University letter forms as well as its symbol. All involved telephone calls to the college offices. To simplify the design, I decided to use only the heads of the Princeton tiger and the Columbia lion, and only the torch from the circa-1952 NYU symbol, an Olympic runner carrying a torch. (NYU and Prudential now use stylized symbols, but the torch I carved, as well as the Prudential Insurance Rock of Gibralter, are both older designs—and were in use at the time my subject was there.)

An essential in the design of an award, unless the overall shape is to be symbolic, is the shape and size of the plaque, because other elements must be fitted to it. I had in mind a rectangle of fairly conventional proportions, and was fortunate to have saved the top of a small stand. It was glued up of 1-in (2.54-cm) maple, 13 $\times$ 17½ in (33 $\times$ 45 cm), with rounded corners and fluted edges, so it required only top sanding to be ready for use. I planned to incise the lettering with a V-tool, and trials on the back of the top showed that it could be carved with a good, clean line, providing, as always, that the V-tool was sharp.

The next step was to lay out the plaque and size the elements. The principal employer of the subject turned out to be Bear, Stearns & Co., which immediately suggested another symbol in rebus form—a back view of the three bears and their visitor, Goldilocks. In an animal anatomy book, I found a head-on view of a Malay tiger and a practically tail-on view of a bear. My family crest is a lion head with tongue out, and this seemed appropriate to the occasion because the subject had attended Columbia, but was forced to leave after a few months (as a result of his father's death), so did not earn his intended law degree there. (Hence the lightning bolt and the displaced final letters of LLB.)

A phone call to the nearest Prudential Insurance man brought several folders, one of which showed the old symbol of the Rock. I designed my own Goldilocks and had all the elements. The arrangement worked out quite simply: three colleges along the top row, three employers along the bottom. However, because the subject had worked for the first two while he was studying nights at NYU, it seemed preferable to place that unit directly beneath the NYU one and connect them with more rebus symbols—a moon for the night study at NYU, and a sun shining on the Rock for the day work, with a two-way arrow connecting them. Thus the major employer could occupy major space at the lower left. (The alternative would be a conven-tional left-to-right arrangement of each line.)

To lay out the bear group involved drawing silhouettes of the bear pose in three sizes and shuffling them one over the other to get a shape that fit the space and still emphasized the "bear sterns." Goldilocks was sized to fit.

To get contrast with the maple, I decided to make parts of the units three-dimensional. This would avoid a confusing welter of incised lines and lend some depth to the panel. Also, I could use a contrasting color of wood—in this case mahogany scraps—except for Goldilocks, who wouln't really have been appropriate in a dark wood. She is of pine. The heads, bear group, torch and Goldilocks were blanked out with a coping saw, then whittled.

Lettering was laid out as simple unserifed letters, except for the subject's name and the college initials, which conform to *their* style. Incising serifs is troublesome, particularly when the lettering is only ¼ in (6.4 mm) tall. Also, all lettering was done in capitals, to get maximum size for carving. Letter carving was done with the V-tool and a light mallet; this gives much better control than carving by hand. It was necessary in some instances, such as periods and short lines running with the grain, to make stop cuts with the knife, and in a few instances to finish an angular meeting point with the knife, but, in general, lettering could be done quite rapidly by this method.

When lettering was completed, the panel was fine-sanded to remove burrs, then given two good sprayed coats of satin varnish. This provides both a surface finish and a stop for the "antiquing," which is done by brushing in a dark stain and wiping it off the surface, as would be done with scrimshaw. It is very important that the lettering be fully varnished, or the stain will run into the grain at the sides and discolor the surface. (I had this problem in one or two places, which later required scraping of the surface in those areas and respraying.) I used, incidentally, a German Beiz sal-ammoniac, water-based stain, walnut in color.

Once all this is done, the emblems, separately spray-varnished, are glued in place, the assembly given a third coat of varnish, then two coats of wax or clear shoe polish. Sign it, add ring hangers on the back, and it's ready to go.

Fig. 138 (left). Templates were cut from heavy paper to size elements and test their locations. This was particularly important in posing the three bears and Goldilocks, and in checking that the torch was not so large as to obscure the lettering.

Fig. 139. Finished emblems ready to be glued into place.

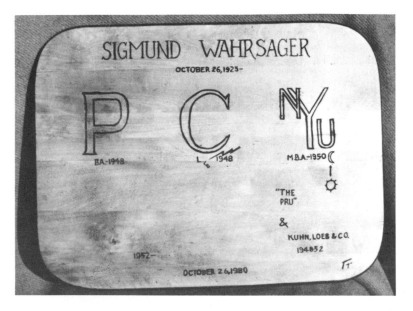

Fig. 140 (above). Lettering was incised with a V-tool on this maple panel, which was then sprayed with two coats of matte varnish. The varnish acted as a stop when stain was put over the surface and then wiped off, as is done in scrimshaw. Fig. 141 (below). Finished panel, showing elements glued in their proper locations. All but Goldilocks are mahogany; she is pine. Finish is matte varnish and wax.

CHAPTER XVIII

Finishing Suggestions

Including gold-leafing, antiquing, metal inlay

THERE ARE A GREAT MANY WAYS TO FINISH relief carvings, of course. Outdoor signs, and panels, usually in pine, basswood or possibly oak, will be painted in most cases, and may even be "antiqued" on an instant basis by beating with chains, scorching slightly with a blowtorch or sandblasting to take off sharp edges. (Some carvers start with old boards to get authenticity; in that case the poorer the finish the more authentic. Poor finish goes with splintered ends and rotten spots—and poor carving. I've known of carvers who buried their products for a week or two to give them antiquity—or dealers who did it after them.) If an outdoor panel is not painted, it should probably be marine-varnished—which means high gloss; matte and satin finishes simply will not hold up in the weather.

With the above exceptions, I prefer a good wood and a natural finish, with low gloss. You can obtain this on good hardwoods simply by oiling and waxing. I have found processed oils such as Danish finish and tung-oil finish to be better than boiled linseed, though more expensive; they're all that's needed on teak, for example, even for constant exposure. Teak will retain its color and finish with such oiling semiannually. And instead of the familiar waxes, which are preferable for something that will be touched or handled frequently, I use Kiwi® neutral shoe polish. It does not turn white or grey in crevices, nor build up with subsequent polishing. (Kiwi is the "wax finish" used in such divergent places as Bali and Sri Lanka.)

Panel carvings can often be improved by antiquing, the application of a slightly darker stain and immediate rub-off, so the darker color is retained only in crevices. This is what happens anyway as a panel ages—dirt collects in crevices and darkens them, thus giving the panel color contrast and greater apparent depth. If you plan to antique, give the panel a couple of coats of spray matte varnish first; it helps seal the pores and prevent instant absorption of the darker stain in cross-grain areas. I have also found very useful the so-called Beiz finishes, based on sal-ammoniac instead of oil, incorporating a wax and apparently obtainable only in Germany. These finishes, like American Minwax®, provide color and polish in a single coat—particularly on soft woods—and can be applied one over the other for special effects and toning.

Signs, nameplates and liturgical carvings are quite common in relief carving, and may require gilding or gold-leafing of anything from lettering to the entire surface. Gilding is actually just another kind of lacquering, and the technique is detailed on the container. Bronzing, coppering and silvering are similar. All can be applied in many tints with spray cans—with a spray-can result. I have done better with rub-on compounds, particularly for various shades of gold. These are apparently gilt in a wax, so careful application with the fingertips and rubbing in improves the finish. Paints, brush or spray, tend to pile up in crevices and show brush marks. They are not durable when exposed to the weather and somehow look synthetic. If used, they must be covered with some sort of finish, such as a polyurethane varnish.

The ultimate in such work is to apply gold leaf, which is ridiculously expensive today. Real gold leaf is about one three-hundredth as thick as a human hair! There is, of course, imitation gold leaf just as there is silver leaf, also an imitation. Imitation gold is readily available in paint and hobby stores, comes in packets containing 5.2 sq ft (.468 sq m) as 25 leaves, each 5½ in (14 cm) square. The imitation gold is thicker than the real thing, harder to pick up, handle and cover an area with, and usually comes in loose sheets separated by thin paper. Imitation gold must be protected or it will tarnish, particularly out of doors. Real gold, these days mostly from West Germany, comes in packets of 25 leaves, 3¼ in square (21 sq cm) totalling 284 sq in (1,832 sq cm). It is actually quite hard to find. It can range from 13½ to 23 karats in purity; real gold is 24 K but has a tendency to split when worked. Woodcarvers use 22 to 23 K gold leaf. Real gold leaf comes either in loose or transfer sheets, the latter held to the backing tissues by jeweller's rouge. The transfer gold is easier to use because it is applied just like a decal, the tissue peeled off after it is applied. It avoids a great deal of fussing with brushes and specialized transfer devices, but is somewhat less economical because parts of sheets may be lost or incorrectly applied.

If you plan to use real gold leaf, the carving should be suited to it. This means selecting a wood that is not too coarse in grain—basswood is ideal—and without undercuts or extremely complex or difficult-to-reach areas. The gold may bridge over such areas or not adhere properly.

The traditional process of applying gold leaf to surfaces, including wood-carvings, is described in exhaustive detail in *Wood Carving*, by Wheeler & Hayward (Sterling), in which the process occupies two entire chapters. Included are meticulous descriptions of how one mixes a special gesso and a special boles, selects proper brushes and knives and how many preparatory coats are to be applied before the gold leaf. Further, there is the necessity of selecting between oil and water application of the leaf, the use of special brushes for free leaves and so on. Actually, the method can be much simpler. Suppliers of gold leaf can provide it, or it can be done as explained to me by Gardner Wood, who has gold-leafed many temple carvings over the past fifteen or more years.

Gardner Wood advises beginning with a relatively dense wood, such as basswood, that requires no filler (oak is obviously a bad choice). If filling is necessary, use a lacquer sealer like Prime®, following the directions on the can. When it dries, sand lightly with very fine or worn sandpaper to get rid of any raised wood fibres. Then cover the surface with gold size, available from the gold-leaf supplier and most paint stores. It is a slow-drying, oil-base size (one brand is Swift's®), and should be brushed on in a thin coat and left overnight. The surface is ready for application of the leaf when tacky—when a dry finger touched to it comes away with a pinging sound, and without picking up any size. (The surface will stay in this state for a day or more under normal conditions.) The gold leaf is simply laid over this tacky surface and pressed down with dry fingertips. Transfer sheets have a blank corner, so the sheet can be picked up without touching the gold. When rubbed down, the transfer tissue can then be readily lifted off. Inevitably, some gold will be wasted, and some missed areas will have to be filled in. To prevent gold adhesion in unwanted areas, dust them with a little talcum powder; to remedy it, just use an ordinary ink eraser.

When covered, the surface must be burnished to remove jeweller's rouge that held the gold to the transfer sheet and to seal it. This is best done with balls of combed cotton rubbed over the surface in a circular polishing motion. If done properly, the surface will immediately show a higher gloss. Following burnishing, any areas that are likely to be abraded—such as the shank of a candlestick or the pushing surface on a door—should be protected. A finish like McClosky® Heirloom varnish will do the job nicely.

A gold-leafed surface is basically ultra-smooth, though it may sometimes be desirable to have a textured surface. Mr. Wood achieves the latter by using a product called Liquid Steel, basically an epoxy containing powdered steel, which can be brushed on the wood surface before gold-leafing. This creates a black surface that can be raked, combed or otherwise textured as desired. It is lightly sanded when dry. Because of the texturing, it is obvious that the application of gold leaf would cause bridging and holes that would show the black surface. To avoid this, the textured surface is sprayed with bronze or another tone. Then gold leaf is applied, rubbed in and burnished. It will leave some voids because of the texturing, but these create an antiqued look.

Gold leaf alone tends to be flat and uniform, so it may be desirable to antique it to bring out depths and shadows. There is available a heavy paste called Rub'n Buff® (American Art Clay Co., Inc., PO Box 68163, Indianapolis, Indiana 46286) available in many art-supply stores in 18 tones of brass, bronze, copper and gold. The paste will stick to any surface, and can be applied by rubbing or by thinning with turpentine and using a brush in difficult areas. Various tones can be applied one over the other to get special effects. It is particularly effective over textured areas, and the more the surface is rubbed the better it gets. The virtue of such texturing is that the surface color can range from a yellow gold to a green in recessed areas. As before, the treated surface should be protected with a good polyurethane varnish if subjected to frequent handling or other unusual wear. Otherwise, gold leaf will stand years of atmospheric wear, requiring only occasional washing with water and a mild soap to remove smog and grime deposits.

On old gunstocks you will find a form of inlay that could be more widely used because it is relatively simple to do. It can be done with silver, brass or copper flat wire or strip, or combinations, and usually takes the form of long cyma curves or scrolls—sometimes with added accents produced by endwise inlay of "spots" of round wire. In India, it was common to decorate small stylized figures of horses, elephants and the like with brass inlay in this way (Figs. 142 and 143), and examination indicates that the brass was formed to desired shapes, simply driven into a wood such as teak, then sanded off until the crushed fibres of wood at the surface and any projecting brass were removed. The entering edge of the brass was slightly wedge-shaped for penetration.

The conventional method of inserting silver and gold is more considerate of the wood. The desired design is laid out on the surface or transferred to

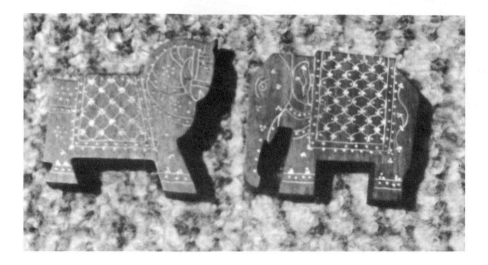

Fig. 142 (above). Horse and elephant are of teak, decorated with brass inserts. The horse, for example, is ¾ × 3 × 3 in (1.9 × 7.6 × 7.6 cm), and wire inserts are 1/64 × 1/32-in (.40 × .79-mm) ribbon. Even the larger spots are made from bits of the same wire, curled up. Fig. 143 (below). Camel and two bullocks are also of teak with brass inserts. Pieces such as these, as well as those in Fig. 142, were made in India years ago, but are probably too costly to produce at today's tourist prices.

it after all but final sanding has been done (so metal dust sanded off later will not penetrate surface crevices). Then a narrow trench is produced along the lines of the design by driving in a thin blade sharpened from both sides like a firmer. These can be made from any thin tempered steel, such as straight X-acto® chisel blades. Blade widths can vary from ¼ in (6.4 mm) down to ¹⁄₁₆ in (1.6 mm), the latter for following curves. These blades should be driven into a depth corresponding with wire or strip width and leave a V-shaped groove as wide at the top as the metal is thick. The metal ribbon is then cut off, formed to shape and driven in progressively, using a light hammer and a dowel. The wire should be just about level with the surface, so light sanding will smoothe it at surface level. If the wire buckles during driving, cut out and replace the buckled portion, since flattening out buckled ribbon and attempting to redrive it usually results in failure and added complication from enlargement of the trench.

In woods such as walnut and teak, the sides of the trench will close in and grip the wire with no problems; but you can use thinned glue in the slot to make sure, or rough the side of the wire ribbon slightly with a file. Make sure that any two pieces of wire that butt together are a good joint, because any gap will be very visible when the work is finished. It may be helpful to file the end of the ribbon at a slight angle in such a case, so the upper portion actually wedges in place as it is driven down. Once the wire is in place, the surface is final-sanded, metal filings brushed and dusted away and the piece is ready for finishing. And any finish will include some moisture that will cause the sides of the trench to swell back and grip the insert tightly.

APPENDIX A

Sharpening Hints

THERE ARE FOUR STEPS TO SHARPENING A TOOL, of which the first, grinding, will probably have been taken by the tool supplier. You should not have to grind a tool unless you break it, nick it badly or resharpen it so often that you wear down the basic included angle. Grinding on modern high-speed wheels is fast but dangerous; you're almost certain to burn the tool end, thus drawing the temper and spoiling the tool.

Whetting and honing are hand operations, done on progressively finer-grained stones, either natural or manufactured. Whetting is done on Washita, a yellowish or greyish stone, or on medium-coarse artificial stone. Honing is done on Arkansas, a white, very hard stone from which "slips" are also made. Slips are the small, shaped stones for taking the feather edge off the inner edge of tools, particularly gouges and V-tools, as well as delivering a final polish to a firmer. Makers and sellers of these stones provide detailed instructions for their use.

Stropping is the final operation, and is exactly like what a barber does on a straight razor. It is done on a leather strop or on a board with strop leather glued to its face. Some small boards have two differing smoothnesses of leather, one with oil and a very fine abrasive such as crocus or tripoli, and the other often with oil alone. While whetting and honing are done edge-first, stropping is done with edge last so the tiny saw teeth on the edge of the blade are aligned. In normal use, stropping is fairly frequent, honing less so and whetting only periodic, depending upon wood hardness, frequency of tool use and your own habits in handling.

Many carvers have recently turned to buffing to replace all three final sharpening operations, using buffing wheels shaped to the tools and a series of buffing compounds such as rouge or tin oxide. This has a tendency to round or shorten the actual cutting edge, and may make it wear longer. Some carvers' also prefer hollow-grinding as done with a razor, which tends to thin the blade angle (normally 30 degrees) at the cutting edge, making it cut faster in soft woods but probably require more frequent sharpening.

The typical movements in hand sharpening and stropping are shown (Figs. 144–145). It is important to spread the wear over the stones and strop to prevent their being worn hollow. Stones should be kept lubricated with thin machine oil, or even a 50-50 mixture of machine oil and kerosene. They should be wiped off and the oil replaced when it turns grey from metal inclusions and dust. Periodically, stones can be washed with benzine or gasoline. Natural stones can be boiled in water with a little baking soda to remove oil and grit. Manufactured stones should not be boiled but rather warmed in an oven.

Note that I use a circular or oval motion in stoning a knife, making certain I get the tip—where most dulling usually occurs in detail carving. Stoning is sketched in *A*, stropping in *C*. Edge sharpness can be tested as in *D* by trying it on the edge of a piece of paper or on the thumbnail; it should cut paper and "stick" on the nail, indicating cutting. To test tip sharpness, try it on a scrap of soft wood. Similar suggestions for sharpening chisels are sketched in *E* and *F*, the use of a slip in *G*. Getting the almost microscopic inner bevel on gouges shown in *G* helps maintain sharpness. Gouges can be sharpened like firmers, but this is tricky because the tool must be rotated at uniform speed while being pushed on the stone; over-rotation will round off corners, while under-rotation will leave them dull. On a gouge, a major dull area can be spotted as a line of light on the tip, *B*. Trickiest to sharpen is the V-tool, because a misshapen edge is easy to get and hard to use. Too thick a

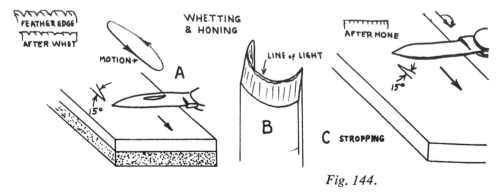

Fig. 144.

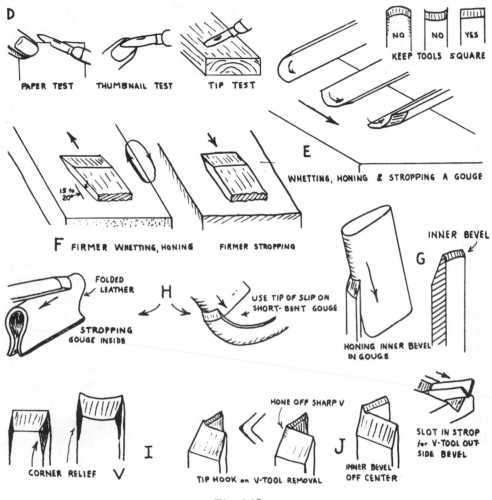

Fig. 145.

tip will tear the wood and may even cause splitting, but too thin an edge will crumble and, again, not cut. Relieving the bottom of the "V" very slightly may be helpful, as is bevelling the edges of a gouge (I).

APPENDIX B

How to Change Size

AVAILABLE DESIGNS ARE OFTEN TOO SMALL, or may not fit the wood you choose. If you can take a good photo of the design or of the subject, it can be projected onto the wood or a piece of paper in the desired enlargement and traced. You can then use elements from several transparencies together. Or you can have prints made to the desired size. Failing these, you can take the original drawing or photo to an art studio and ask them to make a suitably sized photostat (ordinary copiers won't do it: they copy only same size in most cases).

I have used all of these methods, but I usually am working without a negative, so I use one of two methods to get a pattern. The first is the method of squares (Fig. 146). I have a grid of ⅛-in (3.2-mm) inked squares on transparent plastic that I place over the original—say a drawing in this book. If I am doubling size, I draw a similar grid of ¼-in (6.4-mm) squares on paper or the board. If I'm tripling, it's ⅜-in (9.5-mm) squares; if I'm enlarging to 1½ times, it's ³⁄₁₆-in (4.8-mm) squares. Then I copy the design square by square. This is easy, but I become confused among the squares on occasion.

The other method I call point-to-point (Fig. 147) because it resembles the puzzles that children do by drawing a line from number to number. I establish base lines at the side and bottom (or top) of the original, either by drawing them in or putting a square over the original and anchoring it in place. I draw similar base lines on paper or on the panel. Then I locate prominent points, one by one, by getting the horizontal and vertical dimensions of each from the base lines, multiplying each dimension by the multiplying factor and plotting it on the new sketch. To double, I multiply each dimension by two, and so on. This method gets a bit hairy if you want to enlarge 50 percent and have to multiply 1⅞ in (4.8 cm) by 1½ (3.8 cm), but it works well for me since I am reasonably fast and accurate at simple mental arithmetic. When key points are located, simply draw the design between them and fair them in. I find this best for working from a photo or book illustration, on which outlines may not be clear enough for the method of squares.

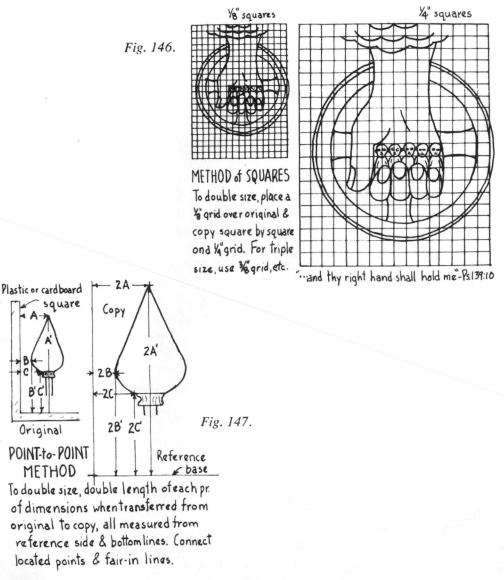

Fig. 146.

⅛" squares

¼" squares

METHOD of SQUARES
To double size, place a
⅛" grid over original &
copy square by square
ond ¼" grid. For triple
size, use ⅜" grid, etc.

"...and thy right hand shall hold me"-Ps.139:10

Plastic or cardboard
square

Copy

Original

2A'

2B' 2C'

Reference
base

Fig. 147.

POINT-to-POINT
METHOD
To double size, double length of each pr.
of dimensions when transferred from
original to copy, all measured from
reference side & bottom lines. Connect
located points & fair-in lines.

Index